COLERIDGE

COLERIDGE

THE CLARK LECTURES 1951-52

by

HUMPHRY HOUSE

SENIOR UNIVERSITY LECTURER IN ENGLISH LITERATURE
AND FELLOW OF WADHAM COLLEGE, OXFORD

DUFOUR

PHILADELPHIA

1965

Library of Congress Catalog Card Number: 65-20490

Printed in Great Britain by Fletcher & Son Ltd., Norwich
for Dufour Editions, Inc., Chester Springs, Pennsylvania

TO
MADELINE
RACHEL
HELEN
AND
JOHN

CONTENTS

CONTENTS: CONTINUED

PREFACE

I wish first to thank the Master and Council of Trinity College, Cambridge, for their invitation to deliver the Clark Lectures, for their hospitality to me during the course, and for the distinction of joining my predecessors in the Lectureship. An over-generous audience, at least appreciating the quotations, converted what might have been an ordeal into a pleasure.

The six chapters of this book contain the substance of the six lectures as they were delivered, but some details of style have been changed, and some sad mistakes put right. In Chapter III the discussion of "Frost at Midnight" has been expanded. In Chapter IV I have rewritten the final paragraphs on "The Ancient Mariner"; and I have added a little new material to Chapter V. Much of the matter in these three chapters derives from an earlier course of lectures given to undergraduates reading the English School at Oxford.

With the permission of the authorities of Trinity I broadcast in the BBC Third Programme, during March 1952, shortened versions of the first two lectures and a compressed treatment of "The Ancient Mariner" and "Kubla Khan": texts of these broadcasts have not been published. I take this opportunity of thanking the many listeners who kindly wrote to me about them.

The chief interest of this book centres on the passages which are now published for the first time from Coleridge's manuscript Note-Books. I first became acquainted with these in 1934 when they belonged to Lord Coleridge, and I was organising, with Professor R. C. Bald, the Coleridge Centenary Exhibition at University College, Exeter. I then made first transcripts of many of the passages quoted here. Some other, familiar, passages are quoted from manuscript with the deliberate purpose of correcting the accepted text of *Anima Poetæ*; but not all my quotations from that selection have been checked against the manuscript. The original Note-Books are now, through the great generosity of the Pilgrim Trust, in the British Museum. I wish to thank Mr. Alwyne Coleridge for permission to quote copyright material. Miss Kathleen Coburn, who is engaged on the immense task of editing the whole series, has gladly let me anticipate small parts of her work; she has also compared my transcripts with her own, so that some of her readings now appear in my texts; and, beyond all this, she has let me tell the dramatic story of "Theodorus Chersites" in Appendix III. I hope I understand "that a grateful mind by owing owes not". To Professor Bald I owe much, not only for his talk at the time of the Exeter Exhibition, but also for giving me a summary, which he then made, of the contents of all the Note-Books, and his key to the manuscript source of every entry in *Anima Poetæ*; these two documents have been invaluable.

In the passages which are printed here from the manuscripts, an attempt has been made to preserve, as far as possible, the punctuation, capitalisation, abbreviations etc. of the originals, so that the note-like character of the material may appear. The recurrent use of an oblique stroke, sometimes in place of a full point, sometimes in place of a comma, is a marked feature of Coleridge's punctuation. Conjectural or illegible words are indicated in the text by square brackets, and are usually mentioned also in the footnotes.

The only other literary manuscripts in which I have ever seen the systematic use of the oblique stroke are the Note-Books of Gerard Manley Hopkins; and this fact, together with certain rather unexpected likenesses in descriptive method, has led me to wonder whether Hopkins may not possibly have seen the Coleridge Note-Books during his boyhood friendship with Ernest Hartley Coleridge.

Many friends, colleagues and pupils—especially Miss Dorothy M. Mercer, Mr. George Forrest, Mr. E. L. Stahl, Mr. James Maxwell and Mr. J. P. Mann—have helped in one way or another. Mr. Hugh Macdonald alone can estimate what I owe to his knowledge and friendship in the whole enterprise.

The full original version of "Dejection: an Ode" is here reprinted with the kind permission of the executors of the late Professor Ernest de Selincourt and of the Clarendon Press.

My wife was deeply involved, very soon after our marriage, in the Exeter Exhibition and its Catalogue; she has endured rehearsals of these lectures and typed the whole text of them: they are therefore dedicated to her, together with our children.

HUMPHRY HOUSE

December, 1952

LIST OF ABBREVIATIONS

Add. MSS: British Museum Additional Manuscripts.

AP: *Anima Poetæ*, From the Unpublished Note-Books of Samuel Taylor Coleridge, Edited by Ernest Hartley Coleridge, 1895.

Bald: R. C. Bald, "Coleridge and *The Ancient Mariner*", *Nineteenth Century Studies*, Collected and Edited by Herbert Davis, William C. De Vane, R. C. Bald, Cornell University Press, 1940.

BL: *Biographia Literaria*, By S. T. Coleridge, Edited with his Aesthetical Essays by J. Shawcross, 2 vols, 1907.

C: *Christabel*, By Samuel Taylor Coleridge, Illustrated by a Facsimile of the Manuscript, and by Textual and other Notes, by Ernest Hartley Coleridge, 1907.

CMC: *Coleridge's Miscellaneous Criticism*, Edited by Thomas Middleton Raysor, 1936.

CSC: *Coleridge's Shakespearean Criticism*, Edited by Thomas Middleton Raysor, 2 vols, 1930.

Gillman: James Gillman, *The Life of Samuel Taylor Coleridge*, 1838. Only Vol. I published.

L: *Letters of Samuel Taylor Coleridge*, Edited by Ernest Hartley Coleridge, 2 vols, 1895.

Lowes: John Livingston Lowes, *The Road to Xanadu*, Revised Edition, London, 1931.

Nethercot: Arthur H. Nethercot, *The Road to Tryermaine*, A Study of... Coleridge's "Christabel", Universityof Chicago Press, 1939.

PW: *The Complete Poetical Works of Samuel Taylor Coleridge* ... Edited ... by Ernest Hartley Coleridge, 2 vols, 1912.

Richards: I. A. Richards, *Coleridge on Imagination*, 1934.

UL: *Unpublished Letters of Samuel Taylor Coleridge*, Edited by Earl Leslie Griggs, 2 vols, 1932.

Warren: *The Rime of the Ancient Mariner*, By Samuel Taylor Coleridge, Illustrated by Alexander Calder, with an Essay by Robert Penn Warren, Reynal and Hitchcock, New York, 1946.

CHAPTER I

THE APPROACH

IT is now a familiar line of approach to say that the outward events of Coleridge's life are of quite secondary importance, and that his history is the history of a mind. He himself can be readily quoted in support of such treatment: as early as 1795 he excused his failure to produce poems for Cottle by saying that he had very little "finger industry", but that his mind was always on "full stretch":[1] in 1796 there is the famous letter to Thelwall, in which he said ". . . but I do not *like* history. Metaphysics and poetry and 'facts of mind' . . . are my darling studies":[2] at the end of 1801 there is the wonderful incidental remark in a Note-Book, that there is "something inherently mean in action" and that the Almighty more or less made a mistake in creating the universe;[3] and in 1822 there is that entry under the very first date of the *Table Talk*: "It is not easy to put me out of countenance, or interrupt the feeling of the time by mere external noise or circumstance". One could make a powerful catena of quotations to show how Coleridge believed that, whatever external circumstance or chance or time might do to him, his mental life and his feelings were normally valuable and inviolable.

There is no doubt that the details of his outward life are often complex or obscure without being correspondingly rewarding; they are repetitive in their pattern and often dull. When, some years ago, a biography was confined to "the limits of a narrative" and claimed to be little more than "a bare chronicle of his questing and

[1] Joseph Cottle, *Reminiscences* (1847), p. 38.
[2] *L*, I, 181; 19 Nov 1796.
[3] MS Note-Book No. 21. Add. MSS 47518, f. 39. See below, pp. 35 and 36 and *AP*, p. 27.

self-tortured pilgrimage through life",[1] it was healthy and proper to protest that the Coleridge one admired and loved was almost completely missing. But now, when the treatment of him as a "mind" has become almost the accepted procedure, it is perhaps time to look at the dangers in it.

By minimising the importance to Coleridge of the external world in which he lived, we run the risk of diverting attention from some of his most characteristic strengths as a writer—from his power of detailed poetic description of objects in nature; from his power of attuning moods of emotion to landscape and movements of weather; of using the shapes and shifts and colours of nature as symbols of emotional and mental states. Even his critical idealism, whether expressed in poems or in his more technical philosophy, is grounded in a minute analysis of the phenomena of sense. He is far more alert and sensitive to the modes in which sense-experience conditions the life of the mind than most technical philosophers.

It is almost more absurd to exalt him as a philosopher who in his youth accidentally wrote "The Ancient Mariner" and "Kubla Khan", than it was, in the older-fashioned way, to lament that a great lyrical poet wantonly atrophied his creative powers by a perverse devotion to German metaphysics. He himself watched this change taking place with minute attention and analysis; but during the critical years 1800–1807 his senses did not fail, and he never failed to record what they reported to him. His quivering alertness to every stimulus of sense was, as I hope to show, the ground of his strengths and of his weaknesses. And this cannot be appreciated if we lift him altogether out of the area of mundane biography. And though, as I have said, it would be easy to make a catena of quotations from his published works, Note-Books and letters, to show his indifference to the usual circumstances of life in their usual hierarchy, it would be just as easy by the same means to demonstrate that external circumstances,

[1] E. K. Chambers, *Samuel Taylor Coleridge* (1938), p. vii.

ordered to his own development, played an essential part. He wrote in one of the autobiographical letters to Poole in 1797 that after his first three years "*all* assisted to form *my particular mind*".[1] Nothing later overthrew that principle.

And there are now other dangers in isolating the value of his "mind" and of his "thought": they are the dangers of making him appear, either retrospectively or prospectively, a figure primarily of historical interest. Retrospectively he is shown as important in the reaction against eighteenth-century mechanism, against utilitarianism and the ethics of enlightened prudence or the pleasure–pain calculus; in reaction against the politics which emphasised rights as opposed to duties, and saw the State as a fortuitous aggregation of atomised individuals. Prospectively he is shown as (what he undoubtedly was) a formative influence on Christian Socialism, on Young England, on the Oxford Movement and also on the Broad Church party—Dean Stanley even said that if only Coleridge had been able to write like Dr. Arnold, what a man he would have been.[2] One rather wonders what Rugby would have been like if Dr. Arnold had been able to write like Coleridge.

Coleridge was indeed one of the great "seminal minds" of the nineteenth century. He is now also being claimed as a father of Existentialism, an anticipator of both Freud and Jung, of the *Gestalt* psychology and so on. I should be the last to deny the value of historical interest in any writer, or to deny that there is any writer who cannot be enriched or illuminated by seeing him in his historical context; but to suppose that Coleridge is now merely or primarily of interest because he revolted against the narrow mechanism or the sentimentalism of the eighteenth century; or because he was the master of F. D. Maurice and Julius Hare; or because he was a mere foreshadow of something more distant to come, and did very inadequately a number of things which have been done much better since, would be, for me, to

[1] *L*, ī, 10.
[2] R. E. Prothero, *Life and Letters of Dean Stanley*, ch. v. I owe this reference to Mr. John Burridge.

repudiate a conviction that has existed, however shifting and growing, for about twenty-five years—the conviction that Coleridge has the one first essential qualification of a great writer, the power of increasing the range and depth and quality of experience in those who read him with care.

To say this is not the same thing as to call him a great artist; the whole business of literary criticism would be far easier if that one hitch could always confidently be made. In certain poems he was a great artist; but his power over our experience is not limited to those poems. It is one of the ironies of his life that he who saw so clearly, and expounded more fully than any English critic before him, the principle of the organic unity of a work of art, should have achieved that unity so rarely: but it is more ironical still that without achieving the unity he should so often, otherwise, have contributed to the very ends which his own principle of unity was designed to serve. Not all great writing is, in the austere monistic way, great art. And much of Coleridge's greatest writing is scattered in Note-Books and Marginalia which even now have not all been published or have not yet received the editing they deserve. On that editing a great deal depends: and it is not merely a matter of selection. It has been said that all that is worth preserving of Coleridge's writing could be printed on fifty pages, but that those fifty pages should be bound in gold. But such precious limitation would entirely fail to reveal him.

One of Coleridge's best editors, Mr. Stephen Potter (whose Nonesuch selection runs to over 700 pages without the notes), is also one of his most valuable interpreters: but his book, *Coleridge and STC*, proceeds by a drastic method. It treats him as a split person: on the one side is "S. T. C.", the character, the ego; on the other is "Coleridge", the personality, the self. All the failures, the delays, the weakness of will, the shattered hopes, the quarrels, the self-pity, the remorse and self-recrimination; the broken family life, the failures of affection, the opium-eating and the drinking; all the muddles about publication, the unfinished works; the protective pomp of manner and self-justification; all the whining and expostulating—all this Mr. Potter attributes to "S. T. C." Against that character he sets the personality "Coleridge", confident in the accuracy of his own self-knowledge, unblinking; drawing on all the resources of ˙ ˙ memory in the act of creation, exploring and expressing the life of a mind of incomparable richness and insight; the personality which approximated to its own ideal of looking forth

calm and sure
From the dread watch-tower of man's absolute self.[1]

Of course, such dual views of Coleridge were current even in his lifetime. Lamb said, after Hazlitt's article in *The Examiner* (8 September 1816): "Such an article is like saluting a man, 'Sir, you are the greatest man I ever saw', and then pulling him by the nose." [2] Carlyle wrote in 1825: "Coleridge is a mass of richest spices, putrefied into a dunghill. I never hear him *tawlk* without feeling ready to worship him, and toss him in a blanket." [3] Sterling said there was a glare in his eye "half unearthly, half morbid".[4] And the contradictions in his personality have been the theme of other writers since. But Mr. Potter applied this dichotomy resolutely as a principle, and used it as an instrument in the critique of Coleridge's writing. In a very perceptive chapter called "Joint Authorship" he shows how the "Estecean" character is liable to appear in all its most unattractive features in the published works, just because the act of publication (being the focus of so many of his moral shortcomings) brought on an awkward self-consciousness, and unsuccessful attempts at ingratiation and

---

[1] "To William Wordsworth", ll. 39–40; *PW*, I, 405, quoted by Potter, p. 113.

[2] Crabb Robinson, *Diary*, quoted by E. V. Lucas, *Life of Charles Lamb* (1905), I, 367.

[3] Letter to John Carlyle, 22 Jan 1825; Froude, *Thomas Carlyle . . . First Forty Years . . .*, ch. xvii.

[4] J. C. Hare's "Sketch of the Author's Life", prefixed to his edition of *Essays and Tales* by John Sterling (1814), I, xxv.

defence. He shows, too, how even in his letters, whenever some really important occasion arises—like thanks for loans of money, reconciliation with his family, birth or death—Coleridge muffs the tone, and becomes lachrymose or sententious: "instead of simplicity there is a chilling excess of feeling". The voice is now the voice of Pecksniff, now that of Micawber. And we might add that there are strains of Stiggins and Chadband too. Contrasted with all this is the spontaneity, freshness and point of Coleridge's unpremeditated writing or talk.

Of course Mr. Potter is far too intelligent not to see that "Coleridge" and "S. T. C." often intermingle; that "Coleridge" is often working on data which only "S. T. C." could have provided; and that one is often discovered commenting on the other. But yet his book, taken together with the other partial or one-sided treatments of Coleridge which are now familiar, suggests that the main task still lies ahead—the task of putting Humpty Dumpty together again. It is a task of portentous difficulty; and this chapter will do no more than propose, very tentatively, three lines of tactical approach to be reconnoitred: 1. The adjustment of initial sympathy. 2. The fuller criticism of Coleridge's various prose. 3. The continuation of the work already in hand on the editing and reinterpretation of his scattered works.

In the first place, an unqualified hostility to the character of "S. T. C." in all its doings imposes a cramping limitation of sympathy. Without some sympathetic acceptance of Coleridge in his worst humiliation—as when he is deceiving Dorothy Wordsworth about what he has written for *The Friend*; or lying about works he says he has just ready for the press; or abusing behind his back the brother before whom he has recently cringed— unless we can face this wickedness, or wrong, or sin (whatever our ethical theory or belief may lead us to call it), our emotional attitude towards Coleridge as a whole will be incomplete, and we shall be partly hamstrung in beginning to interpret much of his greatest work. He was not a glamorous or systematic Romantic sinner who, like Byron or Baudelaire, seized on the idea of evil as a stimulus: he was a genuine sinner, who did what he believed to be wrong against his conscience and his better judgement; he was an important sinner, whose sins were meanness, hypocrisy, self-deceit, the desire for praise where praise was hardly due. Coleridge was a tortured, tearful, weak, self-humiliating sinner, confessing, with abasement:

> Video meliora proboque;
> Deteriora sequor.

It is interesting and extraordinary in him that he admitted his friends to the view of his abasement. We can see that confessed humiliation in many of his letters; and his Note-Books reveal even more that he did not openly confess.

It is a commonplace to say that to pity Coleridge is an impertinence. The most famous statement was Lamb's: Crabb Robinson wrote in his diary:

"In the evening at Charles Lamb's. He was serious, and therefore very interesting. I accidentally made use of the expression 'poor Coleridge!' Lamb corrected me, not angrily, but as if really pained. 'He is', he said, 'a fine fellow in spite of all his faults and weaknesses. Call him Coleridge; I hate *poor*, as applied to such a man. I can't bear to hear such a man pitied'." [1]

But there are many different kinds of pity, of which the carelessly patronising kind, to which Lamb objected, is the least significant. A developed, comprehending pity, so far as we are capable of it, a pity like tragic pity, is needed. The area in which we should pity him, the things for which we should pity him, are beyond our normal emotional scope. This attitude is essential in fully understanding some of Coleridge's most autobiographical poems, such as "Dejection: an Ode"; "The Pains of Sleep"; "To William Wordsworth"; "Youth and Age", and it is an impoverishment of the meaning of

---

[1] 3 Aug 1811; ed. Thomas Sadler (1869), I, 339–40.

those poems to read them with a predetermined resistance to their source in Coleridge's total experience; and that total experience includes all the worst of "S. T. C." Even the more impersonal poems, "The Ancient Mariner" above all, though not by any means to be primarily interpreted or valued by biographical reference, can yet have their meaning enhanced by the most terrible details of biographical knowledge. And if there is one single point from which this proper pity may grow, it is that note added at the end of the uncompleted poem "The Three Graves":

> *"Carmen reliquum in futurum tempus relegatum.* To-morrow! and To-morrow! and To-morrow!"* [1]

In a later chapter it will appear [2] how at critical points in the autobiographical poems it is possible to see in a word or a phrase or a rhythm a sudden expression of emotional weakness of a peculiar kind—implying, often, self-pity—which does not properly belong to the poem as a whole, but is rather an added unexpected gaucherie, with all the appearance of being there through some momentary lapse of control or alertness. It is "S. T. C." intruding on "Coleridge". But in other poems, and in a great deal of the prose, it is not so easy to be certain what is happening and to claim the method of dichotomy as an all-but-infallible instrument.

It is not enough to divide the prose into two main categories of style. On either side of the line there are great varieties; and, moreover, qualities which should, on the theory, be found on one side of it, shift across subtly to the other. Even Coleridge's public prose style is too complex for this instrument to cope with. For one thing, it is not always easy to gauge the quality of pomp in his seriousness; for it is not always pompousness. It would need too many examples, and too long, to establish this fully here. What I mean may, however, be seen in the first paragraph of the Prefatory Note to "The Wanderings of Cain".

This was written for publication in 1828. The situa-

[1] *PW*, I, 284.   [2] See below, p. 139.

tion is one which, in Mr. Potter's terms, belongs entirely to "S. T. C.", not to "Coleridge". A mere fragment of a work, written nearly thirty years before, is to be solemnly included in the Collected Poems. The work is also of a slightly odd kind. The reader is to be wooed to its acceptance. An attitude is struck; there has to be Apology and Explanation, leading to Exculpation.

A prose composition, one not in metre at least, seems *primâ facie* to require explanation or apology. It was written in the year 1798, near Nether Stowey, in Somersetshire, at which place (*sanctum et amabile nomen*! rich by so many associations and recollections) the author had taken up his residence in order to enjoy the society and close neighbourhood of a dear and honoured friend, T. Poole, Esq. The work was to have been written in concert with another, whose name is too venerable within the precincts of genius to be unnecessarily brought into connection with such a trifle, and who was then residing at a small distance from Nether Stowey. The title and subject were suggested by myself, who likewise drew out the scheme and the contents for each of the three books or cantos, of which the work was to consist, and which, the reader is to be informed, was to have been finished in one night! My partner undertook the first canto: I the second: and which ever had *done first*, was to set about the third. Almost thirty years have passed by; yet at this moment I cannot without something more than a smile moot the question which of the two things was the more impracticable, for a mind so eminently original to compose another man's thoughts and fancies, or for a taste so austerely pure and simple to imitate the Death of Abel? Methinks I see his grand and noble countenance as at the moment when having despatched my own portion of the task at full finger-speed, I hastened to him with my manuscript— that look of humourous despondency fixed on his almost blank sheet of paper, and then its silent mock-piteous admission of failure struggling with the sense of the exceeding ridiculousness of the whole scheme—which broke up in a laugh: and the Ancient Mariner was written instead.[1]

The reader determined to be hostile to "S. T. C." could describe the paragraph thus: "It starts off with a build-up of the importance of the author's youth; the mere village where he lived is given the cheap handle of a

[1] *PW*, I, 285–7. See also below, pp. 84–5.

Latin tag: his friends were either 'dear and honoured', fit to be called 'Esquire' or else 'too venerable within the precincts of genius' even to be named. The humble author takes on a composition-race and reaches the winning-post before this anonymous and venerable genius has even started. The victory is enhanced by an echo of Milton's *Areopagitica* and a mention of the 'grand and noble countenance' of the humble author's friend. On top of all this, a large part of the story is, to say the least of it, not entirely true." But is this paragraph just the mouthing of an awkward and solemn humbug? I, at least, am convinced that it is not. In a purely formal way of criticism it is easy to see that the climax—"the exceeding ridiculousness of the whole scheme—which broke up in a laugh"—by jumping into a conversational idiom, would be far less effective without the pomp of the opening. In a personal and present way of criticism it is still easier to see that the phrase "full finger-speed" may be an ironical memory of the denial to Cottle of any "finger industry"; that the last phrase of all, "the Ancient Mariner was written instead", acquires its force, after all that has gone before, by introducing what we, for extraneous reasons, value and love, with a clinching casualness; we are taken by surprise: and there is a persisting surprise of emotion even when the paragraph is known almost by heart. But to acknowledge that these final effects are achieved by the simple rhetoric of contrast takes us nowhere in judging the rest.

How does what is, so obviously, in a way laborious win our sympathy? What makes the tone not offensive? I think it is that the units of rhythm—being both heavy and long—isolate each step in the description, so that each is held up in the air as if for inspection. And the author himself is inspecting the phrases too and shares with the reader a kind of surprise both at the whole situation, at the facts presented and at the story coming together. He is smiling without being mock-pompous or whimsical. By unhappy contrast, however, the final paragraph of this same Prefatory Note falls away into

verbose and stumbling half-confessions, half-conceal-
ments, where not even a suspicion of falsehood glozes
the muddle.

Nobody can possibly pretend that Coleridge's formal
published prose is not very uneven; but again and again
there are passages of uncertain tone where the very
laboriousness wins a peculiar effect otherwise than by
setting off in contrast something sharply and pointedly
said. He manages to be clumsy and illuminating in the
same sentence, so that we smile, not exactly at him or
with him, but yet because of him. He is like an awkward
big grown-up picking up a child who struggles and
protests but somehow enjoys it: the management of the
sentences is too firm to let us drop; we are held; we can't
get away; some of the phrases tickle to pleasure, some
to exasperation: and in the whole process of being swept
off our usual floor we are conscious of a special grip
that we recognise and want again.

He can be at once humbly defensive and revelatory.
Cor ad cor loquitur through hesitancies and half-com-
mittal approaches. And that is often how his real heart
speaks, because he is feeling towards an utterly unknown
reader whom he imagines to be prejudiced against him,
not always because of a persecution feeling or anything
of that kind, but because he is genuinely conscious that
what he is trying to say springs from a complexity of
experience which is exceedingly difficult to present and
may easily be misunderstood. He was a person who felt
that all his most valuable experience was solitary and that
it was scarcely possible to convey it to others in prose
both unimpaired and sympathetically presented.

Still more, in his more technical and theoretical
writing, especially when he is attempting to blend his
own solitary experience with technical philosophical
argument, he is often straining against genuine obstacles
of communication. His well-known defence of his own
parentheses, as necessary to express the very living movement of his thought, is a splendidly adequate defence of
his more buoyant passages;[1] but it does not cover the

[1] *L*, II, 558–9.

23

quality of gritty exertion shown in others. He wrote in a Note-Book, after talking to Sara Hutchinson:

Endeavouring to make the [infinitely beloved Darling[1]] understand all my knowledge I learn the art of making the abstrusest Truths intelligible, & interesting even to the un-learned.[2]

But it was an endeavour, and a lesson to be learnt.

On the other side, the unpremeditated and private prose does reveal, in its own quite different way, the underlying complexities which I have been discussing. They are not all complexities of a single kind, nor do they all find a straight, spontaneous, adequate expression even there. Passages which illustrate this point will be quoted in various later parts of this book.

But one relatively easy passage, quoted at some length, may at once illustrate some of the qualities of the style and also make clearer the kind of pity and sympathy required of us, of which I wrote just now. This is an extract from a Note-Book which has not, I think, been published. It was written at Greta Hall, Keswick, in the year after "Dejection: an Ode": the relevance of its theme to that of the ode will be obvious.

Slanting Pillars of Light, like Ladders up to Heaven, their base always a field of vivid green sunshine// —This is Oct. 19. 1803. Wed. Morn. tomorrow my Birth Day, 31 years of age!— O me! my very heart dies!—This year has been one painful Dream/ I have done nothing!—O for God's sake, let me whip & spur, so that Christmas may not pass without some thing having been done/ —at all events to finish The Men & the Times, & to collect them and all my Newspaper Essays into one Volume/ to collect all my poems, finishing the Vision of the Maid of Orleans, & the Dark Ladie, & make a second Volume/ & to finish Christabel.—I ought too, in common gratitude, to write out my two Tours for Sally Wedgwood/

Oct. 19. 1803. The general Fast Day—and all hearts anxious concerning the Invasion.—A grey Day, windy—the vale, like a place in Faery, with the autumnal Colours, the orange, the red-brown, the crimson, the light yellow, the yet lingering

---

[1] These three words have been inadequately scratched out in the MS.

[2] MS Note-Book No. 21. Add. MSS 47518, f. 32v.

Green, Beeches & Birches, as they were blossoming Fine &
Gold!—& the Sun in slanting pillars, or illuminated small
parcels of mist, or single spots of softest greyish Light, now
racing, now slowly gliding, now stationary/ —the mountains
cloudy—the Lake has been a mirror so very clear, that the
water became almost invisible—& now it rolls in white
Breakers, like a Sea; & the wind snatches up the water, & drifts
it like Snow/ —and now the Rainstorm pelts against my Study
Window! [O Σαρα Σαρα why am I] [1] not happy! Why have
I not an unencumbered Heart! these beloved Books still
before me, this noble Room, the very centre to which a whole
world of beauty converges, the deep reservoir into which all
these streams & currents of lovely Forms flow—my own
mind so populous, so active, so full of noble schemes, so
capable of realizing them/ this heart so loving, so filled with
noble affections—O[Σαρα] [2] wherefore am I not happy! Why
for years have I not enjoyed one pure & sincere pleasure! one
full joy!—one genuine Delight, that rings sharp to the Beat
of the Finger!—‡all cracked, & dull with base Alloy!—Di
Boni! mihi vim et virtutem vel tu [   ] [3], eheu! perdite
[   ] [4] !‡ But still have said to the poetic Feeling when it
has awak'd in the Heart—Go!—come tomorrow.—

A day of Storm/ at dinner an explosion of Temper from the
Sisters/ —a dead Sleep after Dinner/ —the Rhubarb had it's
usual enfeebling-narcotic effect/ I slept again with dreams of
sorrow & pain, tho' not of downright Fright & prostration/ I
was worsted but not conquered—in sorrows and in sadness
& in sore & angry struggles—but not trampled down/ but this
will all come again, if I do not take care.

Storm all night—the wind scourging & lashing the rain,
with the pauses of self-wearying Violence that returns to its
wild work as if maddened by the necessity of the Pause/ I,
half-dozing, list'ning to the same, not without solicitations of
the poetic Feeling, for from ‡ [5] I have written, Oct. 20. 1803,
on Thursday Morning, 40 minutes past 2 o/clock. [6]

It is impossible to treat a passage of this kind by any

---

[1] These words have been cancelled in darker ink, but are legible.

[2] Cancelled, but legible.

[3] About six Latin words here scratched out and also cancelled in
darker ink.

[4] One word scratched out.

[5] Coleridge has used the mark ‡ twice earlier in the passage. so
that his intention is not quite clear.

[6] MS Note-Book No. 21. Add. MSS 47518, ff. 53v–54.

simple, prepared, critical instrument. The expressions of failure and self-blame are there, the regrets over work undone, the pathetic resolutions of amendment, the clutching at Christmas like a straw. If we are making moral judgements, Coleridge comes to the very edge of self-pity, but without toppling over. The whole of these extracts—I take them to be at least three entries in the book, made at different times in the course of about sixteen hours—have a half-achieved unity on which their emotional effect much depends. This all-but unity derives from the method—it is similar to the method used, as we shall see, in the poem "Frost at Midnight"— by which several different kinds of experience are given outwardly in detail and are then drawn in to a centre, first in the room and then in the consciousness. And by this means we are given an extraordinarily living impression of the whole personality, together with its context; of the mind projected outwards into the detail and then contracting onto itself so that the context is back-coloured by the prevailing emotion.

One is surprised over and over again by the combination of delicacy and strength with which Coleridge can handle visual detail in his poems. A passage of this kind shows how this was a normal habit of his mind.

Here too in outline, in the rough, is the kind of personal experience from which there grew his insistence on the distinction between the primary and the secondary imagination. The primary imagination as the "living power and prime agent of all human perception" is here active in perceiving the pillars of light, the mist and the autumnal colours. And the secondary imagination appears, not in its achievement—for the "recreation" is here "rendered impossible"—but in its "essentially vital" activity, as it "*struggles* to idealise and unify". We are watching a half-act of artistic creation. And with Coleridge it is over and over again these wonderful half-acts which exert that power over our experience which we value.

Two more examples will illustrate simultaneously the second and third tactical approaches I have mentioned;

26

both the kind of attention his prose requires, and also the problems which are involved in editing it. This must be done at length in some detail, because the argument entirely depends upon the detail.

Walter Pater's essay on Coleridge in *Appreciations* has, as one of its predominant themes, the morbid element in Coleridge's nature. A string of phrases from it shows the line of thought: "some tendency to disease in the physical temperament"; "a kind of languid visionariness"; "a gift for 'plucking the poisons of self-harm' "; "rich delicate dreaminess"; "the faintness, the continuous dissolution". My next chapter will touch on the question of Coleridge's illness, and on his opium-taking; for they cannot be ignored. But I want now to limit attention to one of the main passages from the prose on which Pater bases his argument.

After talking of Coleridge's "faintness" and "continuous dissolution" having "its own consumptive refinements", he makes the following quotation:

In looking at objects of nature while I am thinking, as at yonder moon, dim-glimmering through the window-pane, I seem rather to be seeking, as it were asking, a symbolical language for something within me, that already and for ever exists, than observing anything new. Even when the latter is the case, yet still I have always an obscure feeling, as if that new phenomenon were the dim awaking of a forgotten or hidden truth of my inner nature. While I was preparing the pen to make this remark, I lost the train of thought which had led me to it.[1]

Pater simply commented on this quotation: "What a distemper of the eye of the mind! What an almost bodily distemper there is in that!"

Pater was writing before the publication of *Anima Poetæ*, and therefore his source for this quotation must have been either James Gillman's unfinished life of Coleridge, published in 1838, or else some extract from it. The text of the passage was printed by Gillman thus:

In looking at objects of nature, while I am thinking, as at yonder moon dim-glimmering through the dewy window-pane,

---

[1] *Appreciations* (second edn. 1890), p. 73.

I seem rather to be seeking, as it were *asking*, a symbolical language for something within me that already and for ever exists, than observing any thing new. Even when that latter is the case, yet still I have always an obscure feeling, as if that new phænomenon were the dim awaking of a forgotten or hidden truth of my inner nature.—It is still interesting as a word, a symbol! It is the λογος, the Creator! and the Evolver! What is the right, the virtuous feeling and consequent action, when a man having long meditated and perceived a certain truth finds another, a foreign writer, who has handled the same with an approximation to the truth, as he had previously conceived it? Joy! Let truth make her voice audible! While I was preparing the pen to write this remark I lost the train of thought which had led me to it. I meant to have asked something else, now forgotten: for the above answers itself—it need·d no new answer, I trust, in my heart.—15th *April*, 1805.[1]

So it appears that Pater wrenched what was for him the crucial sentence:

While I was preparing the pen to make this remark, I lost the train of thought which had led me to it.

entirely out of its context, and attached it to a badly mutilated version of a passage with which it had no connection. And he gave no sign whatever that he was not quoting exactly what Coleridge wrote. What is far worse, the first part of the note justifies no suggestion of "consumptive refinements" or "continuous dissolution". It is a private account of a highly complex mental experience. Coleridge does not define what he has to say too sharply; he is scrupulously careful not to overstate. He *seems* to be seeking; the feeling is *obscure*. He is tentatively exploring one special kind of the wide range of experiences which underlie all forms of philosophical idealism. And when he reaches the end of the first part of the note—the part which Pater silently omits—he reasserts the value of external visible nature, not only to himself but also as the expression of creating power. It leads into a theoretic statement which he was later to link to Plotinus.[2] There is not the slightest trace of

---

[1] Gillman, p. 311, where the date is wrongly given.

[2] See A. E. Powell, *The Romantic Theory of Poetry*, pp. 90–1.

distemper of either mind or body. The whole passage is a magnificent statement of a thought subtly developing from visual experience; and it is a statement with which Pater, if he had given his mind to it, could have truly sympathised. When *Anima Poetæ* was published in 1895 Ernest Hartley Coleridge gave an arrangement of the whole paragraph similar to that of Gillman, only he inserted in the middle of it the word "Now" in square brackets, to provide some kind of appearance of a link between the two halves.[1]

In the manuscript the words "and the Evolver", with which the first part of the matter ends, are squeezed in at the foot of a page. On the turn-over, the word "What", opening the second part of the matter, is slightly indented so as to indicate without question the beginning of a new paragraph. Both notes are dated Saturday Night April 14 1805.[2] But they do not belong together at all in one stream of thought: one deals with the sight of the dim-glimmering moon, and the other with an altogether different cause for an author's rejoicing.

The full editing of Coleridge's Note-Books will involve countless problems of this kind. Not only the presentation of new material, but also the correction and re-presentation of old—and the interpretation of it—are essential for the future understanding of Coleridge as a whole. This tremendous task is already far advanced; it is being done, with unbelievable heroism, by Miss Kathleen Coburn of the University of Toronto.

She has already published some of her preliminary findings in the selection of Coleridge's prose called *Inquiring Spirit*. One of these extracts will illustrate the importance of her re-editing. There can be few sentences from Coleridge's work so often quoted in books of literary criticism, or so often used as the subject of essays or examination questions, as the sentence: "Poetry gives most pleasure when only generally and not per-

[1] *AP*, pp. 136–7.
[2] MS Note-Book No. 17. Add. MSS 47514, ff. 69–69v.

fectly understood". It now appears that the whole of this sentence reads like this:

When no criticism is pretended to, and the Mind in its simplicity gives itself up to a Poem as to a work of nature, Poetry gives most pleasure when only generally and not perfectly understood.[1]

The implications of the sentence are almost completely reversed; for it means that when criticism *is* pretended to, then the pleasure follows in proportion to the understanding. The sentence can no longer be enrolled to support a view of poetry as a kind of vague magic. In *Anima Poetæ*, the vital qualifying words were represented by four dots.[2]

One more example, of a rather different kind, will be enough. There is no author to whom we can more fairly than to Coleridge apply that phrase of Mr. Eliot's— that "his erudition is essential to his originality". The whole of Livingston Lowes's great book *The Road to Xanadu* shows in extraordinary detail what wide and various reading went to form "Kubla Khan" and "The Ancient Mariner". It is a work which can never be superseded, as showing learning contributory to the imagination. But wherever one turns in Coleridge's work one is liable to stumble on evidence which shows how in everything he undertook he was drawing on such resources: it is astonishing to see what the "library cormorant" brought up to the surface for food. One very famous passage of this kind can be clarified by looking into its editing.

Everybody remembers the passage at the beginning of Chapter XV of the *Biographia Literaria* in which he writes of "the greatest genius, that perhaps human nature has yet produced, our *myriad-minded* Shakespeare". To the phrase "myriad-minded", Coleridge added this footnote:

Ἀνὴρ μυριόνους, a phrase which I have borrowed from a Greek monk, who applies it to a Patriarch of Constantinople.

---

[1] *Inquiring Spirit*, A New Presentation of Coleridge from his Published and Unpublished Prose Writings, ed. Kathleen Coburn (1951), p. 156 and note p. 424.   [2] *AP*, p. 5.

I might have said, that I have *reclaimed*, rather than borrowed it: for it seems to belong to Shakespeare, "de jure singulari, et ex privilegio naturæ".[1]

So far everything seems fairly clear; but no sympathetic reader of Coleridge will have failed to look at Shaw-cross's note [2] on this passage, or at the extract from *Anima Poetæ* which it quotes; and there the clarity begins to be clouded over. The text in *Anima Poetæ* [3] reads like this:

ὁ μυριόνους—hyperbole from Naucratius' panegyric of Theodorus Chersites. Shakspere, *item*, ὁ πολλοστὸς καὶ πολυειδὴς τῇ ποικιλοστρόφῳ σοφίᾳ. ὁ μεγαλοφρωνότατος τῆς ἀληθείας κήρυξ. —LORD BACON.

This is most extraordinary; for the punctuation, the lay-out and the choice of type make it appear as if Bacon had actually expressed an opinion of Shakespeare in rather extraordinary Greek; or that Coleridge had somehow persuaded himself that Bacon had done so; or that Coleridge had adapted to Shakespeare a piece of extraordinary Greek which Bacon had written about somebody else. Shawcross was evidently uneasy; but he limited his doubts to a bracketed "sic" after μεγαλο-φρωνότατος. And, to compensate, he made a new error of his own, by putting only a comma after σοφίᾳ, as if the phrases ran together.

In fact, a whole number of slips in transcription and typography have combined to turn Coleridge's wisdom into what looks like folly. The entry in his manuscript Note-Book is actually laid out like this: [4]

'Ο μυριόνους—hyperbole from Naucratius's
Panegyric of Theodorus Studites—Shakespeare?
Item—ο πολλοστὸς καὶ πολυειδὴς τῇ
ποικιλοστρόφῳ σοφίᾳ.

Ο μεγαλοφωνότατος τῆς ἀληθέιας κήρυξ—
Lord Bacon

---

[1] *BL*, II, 13.   [2] *ibid.*, 269.   [3] *AP*, p. 21.
[4] MS Note-Book No. 21. Add. MSS 47518, f. 38v. Breathings and accents follow MS, but contractions have been expanded. See App. III.

31

This was written about fifteen years before the passage in the *Biographia*, and things are as clear as daylight; there are three quite separate Greek phrases: two of them are tentatively to be applied to Shakespeare; then a firm dividing-line is drawn, and the third phrase is intended to be a *description of* Bacon. Shawcross was quite right to doubt the adjective μεγαλοφρωνότατος, for Coleridge never wrote it. The phrase for Bacon means "The great-voiced herald of the truth"; and it has no reference to Shakespeare at all, unless, of course, one happens to believe that the two persons were identical.

All the three phrases, in the riotously compounded Byzantine Greek of the eighth century, are taken from an Encyclical Letter sent out by Naucratius after the death of S. Theodore, usually called Studita, rather than Studites, who never, incidentally, was "a Patriarch of Constantinople".[1] The passages are not there adjacent to each other, though they all come in the opening part of the letter, which consists mainly of exclamatory eulogistic phrases, standing only in apposition. In his Note-Book Coleridge did not use the phrases in the order in which they occurred; and he also adapted their meanings by suppressing parts of the context. The key word μυριόνους was not used by Naucratius absolutely, as Coleridge applied it to Shakespeare, meaning "myriad-minded" in all ways and all places unconditionally, but in the phrase "many-minded in governance watched by God"; and it seems to refer to the ingenuity of S. Theodore in supervising the religious life of monks. And that is removed from Shakespeare. The other wonderfully elaborate phrase to be applied to Shakespeare also has, in Naucratius, a qualification which Coleridge did not note. I hardly dare risk the translation of it, but as it stands in the Note-Book it means some-

[1] *Naucratii Confessoris Encyclica de Obitu Sancti Theodori Studitae*; Migne, *Patrologia Graeca*, XCIX, 1828. Theodore derived his name from the monastery of Studium, of which he was the head. My text is here materially changed from the version of the lecture. Appendix III (p. 167) explains how, with the help of Miss Coburn, this came about.

thing like "complex and multiform in the variously versatile wisdom"; and, with only Coleridge to go by, we well might ask—"In the wisdom of what?" Naucratius wrote that Theodore was "complex and multiform in the variously versatile wisdom of the Spirit". And only God knows whether Shakespeare was truly that. Coleridge has seized the word right out of the context in which he found it, and made it his own for another purpose by altering its syntactical function; he made it a new *kind* of word, and gave it new life in the context of Shakespeare. When he writes in the footnote in *Biographia Literaria* that he has "reclaimed" the word, he is in fact making a peculiar kind of modest understatement: he has re-created it. And that altogether alters the tone of the footnote itself. This is his habit of using words as "no passive tools", but as "organised instruments, reacting on the power which inspirits them".

CHAPTER II

MIND AND PERSONALITY

NOTHING is more common than for writers to take up this phrase "myriad-minded" and apply it to Coleridge himself. It is hardly necessary to say that it cannot be applied to him in anything like the same sense as that in which he applied it to Shakespeare; for of Shakespeare's chameleon-like adaptability in creation Coleridge had scarcely any trace at all. If used of him, the phrase "myriad-minded" must belong partly to the immense range of subjects to which he applied his mind, to his intellectual range and versatility; and partly to what I have called more than once the "complexity of his experience", that is, to the variety of modes in which his own "particular mind" operated both under the stimuli of sense and of emotion, and in its reflections upon itself and on the matter of his reading. But any such separation is only for our convenience: in his concrete daily living his learning, his physical and emotional experience ran concurrently and interpenetrated: it is exactly that which makes the task of seeing him "whole" so difficult.

There could be no clearer or quicker way of making this plain than by describing the two pages of the very Note-Book on which he made the extracts discussed in the last chapter.

The passages from the Encyclical Letter of Naucratius which were to be applied to Shakespeare and Bacon were written at the top of the left-hand page of the book. Beneath them follows a list of names and dates of medieval authors, with notes on the editions of their works to use. Included are Bede, Michael Psellus—who occurs in the gloss to "The Ancient Mariner"—Heloisa and Abelard, Peter Lombard—against whose name

Coleridge adds: "His sentences must needs be a common book"—and John of Salisbury. At the top of the right-hand page are the dates and places of publication of three editions of Bede; and of the third of these, published in Cologne in 1612, Coleridge says: "This last a vile edition". Then immediately follows this entry, which has already been mentioned in passing:

Something inherently mean in action. Even the creation of the universe disturbs my Idea of the Almighty's greatness—would do so, but that I conceive that Thought with him creates.

Then comes the quite isolated phrase, as on page 27 of *Anima Poetæ*:

The great federal Republic of the Universe.

Then appears a stanza of Schiller's poem "Die Worte des Glaubens":

Und ein Gott ist, ein heiliger Wille lebt,
Wie auch der menschliche wanke,
Hoch uber der Zeit und dem Raume webt
Lebendig der höchste Gedanke;
Und ob alles in ewigem Wechsel kreist,
Es beharret im Wechsel ein ruhiger geist [1]

This is followed by a curious little fragment of decorative description of a medieval scene:

So many earles & viscounts, that it were long to rehearse—it was a great beauty to behold the Banners & Standarders waving in the Wind, & horses barded & squires richly armed—[2]

---

[1] Coleridge does not give the source, which was kindly identified for me by Mr. E. L. Stahl. Coleridge's punctuation, capitalisation, etc. are kept, and his text corresponds verbally with the received text as given in e.g. *Schillers Sämtliche Werke* (Tempel–Verlag, Leipzig, ND), Erster Band, *Gedichte*, 212. The stanza might be translated: "And there is a God, a Holy Will is living, however the human will wavers. High above time and space the highest Thought lives and acts. While all revolves in eternal change, one steady spirit persists in this change."

[2] 'Standarders' appears to be the reading. To "bard" a horse is to put on its armour.

And at the foot, continuing on, past the turn-over, to the top of the next page, comes the following:

Strictly one should notice the cases in which opium *restores* the patient to his powers, of breathing, for instance; & those far more numerous in which it only suspends the pain of their Suspension.

Within the compass of two pages of a pocket-book it would be hard to compress a more varied picture of mental life. The contrast was made by Ernest Hartley Coleridge, and has been repeated since, between these Note-Books of Coleridge and the Common-place Book of Milton. In Milton's book everything is systematic; there is the Index Ethicus, the Index Œconimicus, the Index Politicus and so on, entries being made in an orderly fashion in each. With Coleridge everything goes in hugger-mugger as it comes into his head in the course of a day. And in some of the books even that chronological unity is wildly and variously broken up by his habit of leaving blank pages, even blank half-pages, which he suddenly used, sometimes years later, when he seized on whichever Note-Book came readiest to hand. He also transcribed material, with or without revision, from one Note-Book into another. But the entries on these two pages seem to belong in time closely together in a short period at the very end of 1801 or the very beginning of 1802.

The matter of learning starts with those wonderful extracts from an obscure Byzantine monk of the eighth century, with the cross-references to Shakespeare and Bacon; runs through the list of editions of medieval writers to a stanza of Schiller written in the 1790's. The piece of medieval description is rather hard to explain; it may be a quotation, but I have not tried to find its source. The note on the meanness of action is a splendid example of his mixture of wry humour directed against himself with a deep and sincere admiration for a contemplative or speculative life, a sharp double-sided weapon of autobiography. And the note on the effects of opium begins calmly, almost clinically, and shades off into the knowledge of its effects on himself, still firmly put, almost like an epigram, without self-pity or complaint. Cutting right across all this matter like the crossing of a cheque is the almost schoolboyish "gorgeous nonsense" phrase "The great federal Republic of the Universe", which anybody may annexe to Political Theory or Metaphysics or Theology, as he chooses.

These pages alone help to clarify the phrase "complexity of experience", but we may perhaps clarify it further by making first a bare list of some of the (more or less) indisputable physical facts and mental and moral qualities which have to be taken into the account.

Exceedingly acute senses and great sensitivity to all sense-experience.

A highly organised nervous system which reacted both quickly and violently to every stimulus.

An abnormal speed of cerebration, but of rather a peculiar kind.

A habit of close introspection and a remarkable talent for it.

An immensely wide range of reading, and a capacity to understand most technical subjects (excepting mathematics only) as far as they were developed in his time.

A deep longing for mutual love, not realised in his marriage, and only imperfectly and intermittently realised in any other relationships.

Recurrent and, finally, chronic ill-health. Opium and laudanum taken in increasing quantities to relieve pain.

An inability to cope with what presented itself as the plain immediate duty. This can be described in moral terms as either idleness or lack of will-power. But it was coupled with a very exact knowledge of what the immediate duty was.

This list of items demands or suggests no obvious treatment in either chronological or any other order of priority. But the illness and opium make an urgent claim on that initial sympathy of which I have already spoken. The ill-health centred mainly on two nameable disorders, rheumatism in various forms and some kind of dysentery: Coleridge called it alternatively "my bowel-complaint". There is a history of recurrent rheumatism from childhood, first after sleeping out in wet fields beside the Otter, after the quarrel with his brother. Then at Christ's Hospital, after swimming in his clothes, he had what he called "Rheumatic Fever"; but I am advised that we should now call this a serious influenza with rheumatism. Next came a violent attack of rheumatism at Cambridge, caused, he thought, by the dampness of his Jesus rooms. In 1795 he wrote to Cottle:

A devil, a very devil, has got possession of my left temple, eye, cheek, jaw, throat and shoulder. I cannot see you this evening. I write in agony.[1]

In November 1796 we hear of violent neuralgia and further illness the next month. The illness at "Kubla Khan" time was an attack of dysentery. In September 1799 he reported to Southey:

A fit of the Rheumatism laid hold of me from the small of my back down to the calves of my Legs, shooting thro' me like hot arrows headed with adder's Teeth: since my Rheumatic Fever at school I have suffered nothing like it![2]

In 1800 the tendency to rheumatism was increased by the move to the damp climate of the Lakes; at the end of June or early July he was seriously ill for a fortnight with rheumatism and fever, which left his eyes inflamed; at the end of the year he was very ill with dysentery followed by boils. At the beginning of 1801 there was another attack of fever and rheumatism: by May, he had swollen knees and knotty fingers. From then onwards such illness was too normal to recount.

With anybody such illness and such pain would bring failures and distresses, as to Coleridge. But with him illness had other effects besides: it helped to reveal himself to himself; it sharpened his pleasures and pains in all areas of his life. He wrote after one attack: "My new and tender health is all over me like a voluptuous

[1] [July–August], 1795. Joseph Cottle, *Reminiscences* (1847), p. 37.
[2] *UL*, I, 127.

feeling." [1] On 15 October 1799 he gave an account of himself which leads us further towards understanding:

I am harassed with the rheumatism in my head and shoulders, not without arm-and-thigh-twitches—but when the pain intermits it leaves my sensitive frame *so* sensitive! My enjoyments are so deep, of the fire, of the candle, of the thought I am thinking, of the old folio I am reading, and the silence of the silent house is so *most and very* delightful, that upon my soul! the rheumatism is no such bad thing as *people make for*. And yet I have and do suffer from it, in much pain and sleep-lessness and often sick at stomach. . . .[2]

Illness intensified his delight in things external to himself, and sharpened his attention and focus to detail.

Novemb. 20th. Midnight.—O after what a day of distempered Sleeps, out of which I woke, all sense of Time & Circumstance utterly lost/ of fever, rheumatic pain, & loads of stomach-sickness.—I get up/ am calm, like one *lownded* [3] —/ as I lifted up the Sash, & looked out at the Sky, for the first minute I thought it all dark, a starless Sky; the wind, all the summer swell lost, & the winter Hollowness & Whistle not yet come, mixed it's sea-like solemn roars with *the Rustle* from the yet remaining half dry Leaves on all the Trees—/ —but I looked again at the sky—& there were many stars, so dim & dingy that they might have put into Paracelsus's Fancy his whim of the Astra tenebricosa, that radiated cold & darkness, with hollow rays, tube-like as Hairs, ensheathing the rays of Light & Heat, & so producing cold & darkness—
Monday Morning, 9 o clock—Cold Rain in the valley, which is Snow upon the mountains. [4]

The Note-Books of 1800 and the period immediately following, that is, at the beginning of the major break-down of his health, are those which contain some of his most beautiful and "inseeing" descriptive prose, as later quotations will show.

But illness also, by making him the critic and analyst

[1] Joseph Cottle, *Reminiscences* (1847), p. 168.   [2] *L*, I, 307–8.
[3] Cf. *L*, I, 400 (26 Aug 1802): "I was sheltered (in the phrase of the country, *lownded*) in a sort of natural porch." See J. Wright, *English Dialect Dictionary*, s.v. "lown".
[4] MS Note-Book No. 21. Add. MSS 47518, ff. 86v–87.

of his own pain, gave an entirely new direction and stimulus to his philosophical thinking. There is no more playing with ideas and systems. When he wrote that "sickness and some other and worse afflictions first forced me into downright metaphysics",[1] he meant that the starting-point of the review of his opinions in those critical years was psychological; that the main method of his psychology was introspection; and that ill-health started him in dead earnest on the "abstruse research" which he saw in one mood as stealing from his own nature "all the natural man". And this, in turn, played back adversely on his health:

Metaphysics make all one's thoughts equally corrosive on the body, by the habit of making momently and common thoughts the subjects of uncommon interest and intellectual energy.[2]

Though Coleridge may often in his letters play up his illness as his excuse for failures of immediate duty, he does not cultivate and foster it as a subject of romantic interest and concern. He may often use it as a pistol for extorting pity; but he is not a deliberate collector of firearms. Without ill-health, much of the direction of his thought and the quality of his writing would have been different: but we are concerned with the Coleridge that we have; and illness, both outwardly and inwardly, contributed to make him, even to reveal some of his strengths.

Nor did he ever build up his opium-taking as a virtue of psychological and romantic experimentalism; he never failed to deplore it.

I have never loved evil for its own sake, no nor ever sought pleasure for its own sake, but only as the means of escaping from pains that coiled round my mental powers as a serpent around the body and wings of an eagle! *My sole sensuality was not to be in pain!* [3]

---

[1] *L*, I, 378; see pp. 46–7 below.

[2] *AP*, p. 23; text corrected from MS Note-Book No. 8. Add. MSS 47505, f. 47. "Momently" seems to be the correct reading.

[3] Lucy E. Watson, *Coleridge at Highgate* (1925), p. 22. Mrs. Watson was Dr. James Gillman's granddaughter.

and

> ... when I am alone, the horrors I have suffered from laudanum, the degradation, the blighted utility, almost overwhelm me.[1]

One of the idealised self-portraits in *The Friend* sets up the ideal of feeling and character of which he never quite lost sight:

> Sickness, 'tis true,
> Whole years of weary days, besieged him close,
> Even to the gates and inlets of his life!
> But it is true, no less, that strenuous, firm,
> And with a natural gladness, he maintained
> The citadel unconquered, and in joy
> Was strong to follow the delightful Muse.
>
> ... Yea, oft alone,
> Piercing the long-neglected holy cave,
> The haunt obscure of old Philosophy,
> He bade with lifted torch its starry walls
> Sparkle, as erst they sparkled to the flame
> Of odorous lamps tended by Saint and Sage.[2]

Inseparable from the problems of health and opium are the problems of his emotional life, and the breakdown of his marriage. The failure of that particular marriage to Sara Fricker is of less importance than the general emotional context within which it was set. He married her on a theory, as a very young man; and all the evidence—both that of the husband and wife themselves, and that of third parties—shows that, though she was in many ways a good woman and might have made many a man a good wife, she was an impossible wife for Coleridge.

But yet the failure of the marriage became the occasion of his explorations of his own emotional nature and intensified the consciousness of his own unique identity, his "selfhood". He exemplified and expressed with extraordinary clarity a paradox which underlies all

[1] Lucy E. Watson, *Coleridge at Highgate* (1925), p. 25 and *L*, II, 269.
[2] "A Tombless Epitaph", ll. 14–20, 28–33; *PW*, I, 413–14.

deep human relationships—that in proportion as the desire is strong to be passionately united in all things to somebody else, so must the recognition grow, in area after area of conquest, that in the last resort such union is impossible. He sees the paradox clearly when he writes:

The unspeakable comfort to a good man's mind, nay, even to a criminal, to be *understood*—to have some one that understands one—and who does not feel that, on earth, no one does? The hope of this, always more or less disappointed, gives the passion to friendship.[1]

The intense consciousness of personal identity has its counterpart in a greater awareness of the difference of others:

In natural objects we feel ourselves, or think of ourselves, only by *likenesses*—among men, too often by *differences*. Hence the soothing, love-kindling effect of rural nature—the bad passions of human societies. And why is difference linked with hatred?[2]

Even in daily living, the sense of likeness and sympathy with natural objects forced him to see that the sympathy could be truly felt only when he was alone:

Monday, Oct. 24. 1803. I walked with Southey & Hazlitt thro' Borrodale into Watendlath, & so home to a late Dinner. Of course it was to me a mere walk; for I must be alone, if either my Imagination or Heart are to be excited or enriched. Yet even so I worshipped with deep feeling the grand outline & perpetual Forms, that are the guardians of Borrodale, & the presiding Majesty, yea, the very Soul of Keswick.[3]

He then goes into a long discussion of what the effect would be if Borrowdale were re-arranged.

It is easy and possibly just, in socially moral terms, to blame Coleridge for his quarrels with Wordsworth; but

[1] *AP*, p. 24.
[2] *ibid.*, p. 25; this passage seems to be close in date to that just quoted from *AP*, p. 24—Oct 1802.
[3] MS Note-Book No. 21. Add. MSS 47518, f. 71. He calls his Note-Books "my only confidants" (*AP*, p. 189).

42

it is important to see a moment of heart-sundering *difference* over this very question of attitudes to Nature:

A most unpleasant Dispute with W. & Hazlitt Wednesday afternoon, Oct. 26. 1803.—I spoke, I fear too contemptuously —but they spoke so irreverently so malignantly of the Divine Wisdom, that it overset me. Hazlitt how easily roused to Rage & Hatred, self-projected/ but who shall find the Force that can drag him up out of the Depth into one expression of Kindness —into the shewing of one Gleam of the Light of Love on his Countenance.—Peace be with *him*!—But *thou*, dearest Wordsworth—and what if Ray, Durham, Paley, have carried the observation of the aptitudes of Things too far, too habitu- ally—into Pedantry?—O how many worse Pedantries! how few so harmless with so much efficient Good! = Dear William, pardon Pedantry in others & avoid it in yourself, instead of scoffing & reviling at Pedantry in good men in a good cause & *becoming* a Pedant yourself in a bad cause—even by that very act becoming one!—But surely always to look at the super- ficies of Objects for the purpose of taking Delight in their Beauty, & sympathy with their real or imagined Life, is as deleterious to the Health & manhood of Intellect, as always to be peering & unravelling Contrivances may be to the simplicity of the affections, the grandeur & unity of the Imagination.— O dearest William! Would Ray, or Durham, have spoken of God as you spoke of Nature? [1]

It would be hard to work out all the implications of that; it must now be enough to see how at a crucial point, not by a difference of opinion, but by a funda- mental failure of attunement in feeling, Coleridge might suddenly and startlingly find himself thrown back into a painful sense of his own isolation. He was admittedly a hyperbolist, not a good maker of allowances. But it was only through such experiences as this that he came to some of his own most valuable moments of insight.

Coleridge never found in human affairs a working compromise between the desire for an absolute love with perfect sympathy and the admission that such absolutes are impossible. A wife who shared the recog-

[1] Text here from MS Note-Book No. 21. Add. MSS 47518, ff. 73v– 74; my text differs slightly from that in *AP*, p. 35, but in the lecture as delivered I introduced two serious errors.

43

nition of the paradox might have done much for him; but his own recognition of it was an essential ground of his religion ; and it reinforced the Platonic strain in his thought which found its fullest poetic expression in "Constancy to an Ideal Object" in 1826. He failed to live always at that level; and in practice denied his best insight.

The daily expressions of the need for love—"O Sara Sara wherefore am I not happy!" or "My illness would not materially diminish my Happiness, if I were House-mate with Love"—are often distracted and terrible, especially because they often accompanied acute physical pain and the knowledge of things undone; but running through them all is the constant urge to explain or supersede, the unremitting self-exploration without which his criticism, for instance, would have been impossible. By living through a hell of isolation, or a limbo of lost identity, he came to discover what part the unconscious may play in art and life.

Though one should unite poetry, draftsman's skill, and music, the greater and perhaps, nobler, certainly *all* the subtler, parts of one's nature must be *solitary*. Man exists herein to himself and to God alone—yea! in how much only to God! how much lies *below* his own consciousness.[1]

In all Coleridge's accounts of his own mental experience none deserve more attention than those in which he speaks of the "streamy nature of association, which thinking curbs and rudders". In these "ten pregnant words" Lowes found the most adequate description of the "fund-amental fact of mind" in the creation of the "Mariner" and "Kubla Khan".[2] The first passage to deal with this streaminess is printed in *Anima Poetæ* on page 55; but I give here the full text from manuscript:

I will at least make the attempt to explain to myself the Origin of Moral Evil from the *streamy* Nature of Association, which Thinking=Reason, curbs & rudders, how this comes to be so difficult/ Do not the bad Passions in Dreams throw

[1] *AP*, p. 31.   [2] Lowes, p. 72.

light and shew of proof upon this Hypothesis?—Explain those bad Passions, & I shall gain Light, I am sure.—A Clue! a Clue!—a Hecatomb a-la Pythagoras if it unlabyrinths me.—Dec 28, 1803—[1]

This is substantially the same text as in *Anima Poetæ*, except that "=Reason" after "Thinking" is omitted there. At this date and in this context the word probably has no intended special distinction from the "Understanding". But the point to bring out now is that in all these places where Coleridge mentions the "streamy" nature of association he mentions it in connection either with the origin of moral evil in general, or explicitly with his own failures to carry on with the obvious duty before him. He ought to have been annotating the margins of Malthus's *Essay on the Principles of Population* —the very copy is in the British Museum to witness the truth of what he says; his annotations, which were apparently designed to help Southey review the book, suddenly stop.

I had begun and found it pleasant. Why did I neglect it? Because I ought not to have done this. The same applies to the reading and writing of letters, essays, etc. Surely this is well worth a serious analysis, that, by understanding, I may attempt to heal it. For it is a deep and wide disease in my moral nature, at once elm-and-oak-rooted. Is it love of liberty, of spontaneity or what? These all express, but do not explain the fact.[2]

After scouting a sophistical connection of these neglects of duty with the associative memory of the "pain roused from the commands of parents and schoolmasters", he returns to the idea that the defect is to be attributed wholly to "the streamy nature of the associative faculty", and that it is most evident in people like Hartley and himself who are "most reverie-ish and streamy".[3]

Now, if Lowes was right in finding in this streaminess of association the very process by which the multiform imagery of "The Ancient Mariner" and "Kubla Khan"

[1] MS Note-Book No. 16. Add. MSS 47513, f. 48.
[2] *AP*, p. 64.   [3] *ibid.*, pp. 65–6.

came up from memory to the surface of Coleridge's mind in the act of composition, there could hardly be a more startling example of how part of his greatest strength and part of his greatest weakness derived from the same mental source. Lowes's treatment of the matter is further discussed in my Chapter VI. But even apart from those two poems, there can be no question that it was by this swift and facile combination of diverse material from his observation and enormous reading that Coleridge achieved his quite exceptional brilliance as an extempore talker and his fertility of image and illustration in his unpremeditated writing; that facility will appear in the descriptive prose I shall quote later.

But this very fertility could be suicidal; it was not only that the stream of association was not always curbed and ruddered by thinking; but that thoughts themselves competed:

If one thought leads to another, so often does it blot out another . . . my thoughts crowd each other to death.[1]

Moreover, the free activity of Coleridge's private mind was a direct cause of his frequent failures of style in his more formal public utterance. Faced with any special occasion, he had to gather himself together out of the current stream and constitute himself afresh to meet the demand of the outside world upon him. It mattered little whether he did so in a hurry or only after long delay; the resulting writer was an *ad hoc* construct, and that construct tended to be some type or other defined by function or by moral attitude, now the dutiful younger brother, now the perfect responsible godfather, now the family man and horticulturalist, now the humble author.

Once his illness and emotional frustration had established themselves as the norm of his daily life, *they* tended to govern the current stream of association; then even poetry seemed to be an external demand, even the poet had to make the effort to reconstitute himself afresh.

. . . I wished to force myself out of metaphysical trains of thought, which, when I wished to write a poem, beat up game

[1] *AP*, p. 189.

of far other kind. Instead of a covey of poetic partridges with whirring wings of music, or wild ducks *shaping* their rapid flight in forms always regular (a still better image of verse), up came a metaphysical bustard, urging its slow, heavy, laborious, earth-skimming flight over dreary and level wastes. To have done with poetical prose (which is a very vile Olio), sickness and some other and worse afflictions first forced me into downright metaphysics. For I believe that by nature I have more of the poet in me. . . .[1]

This famous passage serves as a pivot on which to turn to the next important theme. For though the letter jokingly repudiates what it calls "poetical prose", it has achieved, in the three kinds of bird and their three kinds of flight, clear, precise, fully realised images for the mental moods of which he is speaking. The paragraph is working (as so much of the best prose is) through the mind's processes from the less full to the fuller expression of its purpose. But the clarity of physical vision, and the expression of that vision, is what needs to be stressed. In 1797 he wrote to Thomas Poole, on 16 October:

My mind had been habituated *to the Vast* and I never regarded *my senses* in any way as the criteria of my belief.[2]

That sentence has been quoted over and over again as if it were the most fitting and almost adequate introduction to the study of Coleridge's mind and habits of vision; but it leads people to forget that he also wrote that one of his greatest qualities was "delight in little things", the kind of delight which belonged to "the buoyant child surviving in the man".[3] The selections from the Note-Books given in *Anima Poetæ*, and even in *Inquiring Spirit*, do not fairly represent the frequency of such entries as this:

Black round Ink-spots from 5 to 18 in the decaying Leaf of the Sycamore.[4]

---

[1] *L*, I, 378; to W. Sotheby, 19 July 1802. [2] *ibid.*, 16.
[3] "The Blossoming of the Solitary Date-Tree", ll. 50–1 ; *PW*, I, 396.
[4] MS Note-Book No. 21. Add. MSS 47518, f. 56. This entry follows immediately that about the "eye of a Brobdignag", quoted below, p. 56.

He was even a rival to Hopkins in the search for bye-ways beauty—

What a beautiful thing urine is, in a Pot, brown yellow, transpicuous, the Image diamond shaped of the Candle in it; especially as it now appeared, I having emptied the Snuffers into it, & the Snuff floating about, & painting all-shaped Shadows on the Bottom.[1]

The more one reads Coleridge's descriptions and dwells on them, the less easy it is to be convinced that he ever needed Dorothy Wordsworth as his tutor in seeing.[2] The external evidence fails to make the matter clear, for the majority of Coleridge's detailed descriptions, whether in verse or prose, were written during or after the time of living side by side with the Wordsworths at Nether Stowey and Alfoxden. Except for the material from books, nearly all the entries in the earliest Note-Book (called the "Gutch Memorandum Book"), which was the main source for Lowes's recovery of the reading which lay behind "Kubla Khan" and the "Mariner", are dashed down in a sort of telegraphese, as notes proper are: there are no set and developed descriptions of detail, though there are flashes of detail caught—

& his eyes & the tears in them, how they glittered in the Moonlight![3]

They were Hartley's eyes, which came in at the ending of "The Nightingale". And, even so, many of these entries belong to the Nether Stowey time. The more set descriptions—and indeed the development of the Note-Books generally from telegraphic jottings to a mixture of short and long—begin with the visit to Germany in 1798–99. For Coleridge as for others, travel abroad stimulated the habit of journalising, and we begin to get entries like this:

---

[1] MS Note-Book No. 16. Add. MSS 47513, ff. 47–47v. Coleridge wrote "of the" twice.

[2] See below, pp. 123–4.

[3] The place of this in its context can be seen in *Coleridge, Select Poetry and Prose*, ed. Stephen Potter (Nonesuch) p. 156 and Lowes, p. 8.

Tuesday Night. [Sept] 18th 1798.

Over what place does the Moon hang to your eye, my dearest Sara? To me it hangs over the left bank of the Elbe, and a long trembling road of moonlight comes transversely/ from the left bank, reaches the stern of our Vessel, & there it ends.[1]

and later on the same page the entry goes on in a journalising way:

Chester was ill the Whole time—Wordsworth shockingly ill!—Miss Wordsworth worst of all—vomiting & groaning & crying the whole time!—And I the whole time as well as I ever was—neither sick or giddy. The sea rolled rather high, but I found the motion pleasant to me.

Both these parts of the entry were slightly modified for re-writing in a letter to Mrs. Coleridge dated from Hamburg on 19 September.[2] The first piece, entirely refurbished with various padding and additions, did public duty in "Satyrane's Letters" I, in *The Friend* No. 14 in November 1809, and reappeared yet again in the *Biographia*.[3] But the phrase "the long trembling road of moonlight" lasted unaltered through every representation. Coleridge wrote to his wife from Germany on 14 January 1799, when he was trying to give her "some idea of Ratzeburg": "I am a wretched describer".[4] And so he was, in a situation where the modern equivalent act would be to send a few photograph post-cards of the place: but he was practising; and the description of Ratzeburg in "Satyrane's Letters" III is an improvement on that sent to his wife. He was later capable of sustained and organised description of a high order when he needed to bring a wider sweep of landscape under his own special vision, and these German exercises played their part in training him to that organisation. A single example, which comes just after the date 5 February 1806, will illustrate the developed style:

To conceive an idea of Olevano you must first imagine a round bason formed by a circle of mountains, the diameter of

---

[1] MS Note-Book No. 3. Add. MSS 47498, f. 1.   [2] *L*, I, 259.
[3] *BL*, II, 143–4.   [4] *L*, I, 273–4; *Cf. BL*, II, 166–7.

the Valley about 15 or 16 miles. These mountains all connected and one; but of very various heights, and the lines in which they sink and rise of various Sweep and Form, sometimes so high as to have no visible superior behind, sometimes letting in upon the Plain one Step above them from behind, sometimes two, and three; and in one place behind the third a bald bright Skull of a mountain (for the Snow that wholly covered it lay so smooth & shone so bright in the Sun, that the whole suggested the idea of a polished Skull, and the snow seeming rather a property or attribute than an accident or adjunct rendered the baldness more intense rather than diminished it. The other higher mountains that looked in from behind on the bason with more or less command were lit up with snow-relicts, scarcely distinguishable from Sunshine on bare and moist rock opposed to deep Shade, save when (as often happened) both the one and the other were seen at the same time, when they formed one of the gentlest diversities possible and yet the distinction evident and almost obvious.[1]

The motives for Coleridge's writing down descriptions in his Note-Books varied very much indeed. A number of those in the Gutch book do seem to have been made without question as memoranda for images in poetry, though not necessarily for specific poems, or at least for the poems in which they were later used. One of Lowes's main arguments is that things appeared in "The Ancient Mariner" and "Kubla Khan" which the evidence suggests were intended for some other poem. But there are items which had no such later use, though apparently noted for uses of that kind.

An abrupt beginning followed by an even and majestic greatness compared to the Launching of a Ship, which after sails on in a steady breeze.

The Infant playing with its mother's Shadow—

Rocking its little sister's cradle and singing to her with inarticulate voice.—

The flat pink-colour'd stone painted over in jagged circles and strange parallelograms with the greenish black-spotted lichens.—[2]

In later books, too, there are notes which were actually

[1] MS Note-Book No. 16. Add. MSS 47513, ff. 106v–107v.

[2] Lowes, p. 455.

used in poems. A straightforward and simple instance
occurs in the verses called "Inscription for a Fountain on a
Heath", of 1802. After a wish that the Spring may
long "send up cold waters to the traveller", the verses
continue:

> Nor ever cease
> Yon tiny cone of sand its soundless dance,
> Which at the bottom, like a Fairy's Page,
> As merry and no taller, dances still,
> Nor wrinkles the smooth surface of the Fount.[1]

The prose source of this is given in *Anima Poetæ*:

> The spring with the little tiny cone of loose sand ever rising
> and sinking at the bottom, but it's surface without a wrinkle.[2]

Nobody would dispute that the verses, by introducing
the conventionally fanciful "Fairy's Page", have reduced
the directness of the original vision; but that the introduction of the "soundless dance", and the repetition in
"dances still", have enhanced the sense of life and of the
continuity in the life of the spring.

In passing, it is interesting to compare this with Tennyson's line in "Balin and Balan", in the *Idylls*:

> . . . the spring, that down,
> From underneath a plume of lady-fern,
> Sang, and the sand danced at the bottom of it.

Of which Mr. G. M. Young has said:

> It does not matter whether you have ever seen that or not.
> If you have not, you know now exactly what it looks like. If
> you have, the words will keep it in your memory far more
> vividly than any recollection of your own.[3]

But, alas, both parts of that comment seem to me untrue,
and Tennyson, so often praised for his *accuracy* of vision
and description (that quality also being typical of his
near-pre-Raphaelite age), has to yield here to Coleridge
in that very quality.

There were in my boyhood two springs which on my

---

[1] *PW*, I, 381–2, ll. 8–12.　　[2] *AP*, p. 17, checked from MS.
[3] "The Age of Tennyson", *To-Day and Yesterday*, p. 52.

walks I used over and over again to visit. At one, the water gushed out from the side of a steep hill and fell *down* through foliage into a pool at the bottom, whence the stream then flowed. The other spring was a small neatly formed basin in the middle of a marshy meadow, with its bottom covered by the finest sand. The water bubbled *up* from beneath and "the sand danced at the bottom of it". In memory, Tennyson has confused my two springs; a spring sending its water *down* would churn up the sand rather indiscriminately, if there were any sand. And it is Coleridge who has, ever since, kept my spring in the meadow vividly in memory.

But there is one further point about that prose note of Coleridge's about the spring: in the original Note-Book entry the words as given in *Anima Poetæ* are followed at once by the initials: "W.W. M.H. D.W. S.H." [1] The observation is emotionally linked to William and Dorothy Wordsworth and Mary and Sara Hutchinson. But this important emotional element in the original experience is suppressed in the resulting verses. It looks rather as if Coleridge noted it originally for the pure reason that it fixed something he had enjoyed in the company of his four dearest friends, and perhaps used it in the verses as an afterthought. [2]

In other entries, the intention to use imagery in poems is rather plainer. For instance:

Images. Shadow of the Tree in the ruffled water distinguishable from the Breeze on the water only by it's stationariness.— In clear water over an uneven channel, as in the Greta behind my House, a huge *Boa* convolvulus—an enormous Adder/ — at other time, the waving Sword of Fire of the Cherub over Paradise. [3]

But his descriptions by images are sometimes classificatory, as if to fix in the mind different kinds of visibilia within a general class. For example:

[1] MS Note-Book No. 21, f. 32.
[2] For the place of affection in Coleridge's theory of association and memory, see below, pp. 146–8.
[3] MS Note-Book No. 21. Add. MSS 47518, f. 56.

Weeds forming three beautiful Clouds in the water among weeds of distinct vegetable character—an appearance of down, jelly, & cloud, combined—most like the Cloud of Precipitation in some chemical Decomp.[1]

Or this note on five kinds of waterfall:

An Apron, of tressy water/ 2. a steep Slope of leaping billowy water/ 3. a grand Plunge, an arch of water/ 4 a long Elbow of a narrow Torrent, with many a plunging water-break/ 5 & last a direct perpendicular fall adown a smooth Rock, which nowhere projecting is passively parallel with the stream.[2]

This implies a kind of organised and detailed watching with which he has not always been credited; but the classificatory purpose belongs with his adaptation of a waterfall to emotional experience:

Repose after agitation is like the pool under a waterfall, which the waterfall has made.

But the sweet rhythm of that sentence is a product of his grandson's editing![3]

At other times the descriptions by imagery are explorations, attempts to catch just a particular conjunction of things seen, a moment of special vision that will never come again: in this case not a moment in a flash, but a distended moment, as the moon is going down:

Thursday Morning, 40 minutes past One o'clock—a perfect calm—now & then a breeze shakes the heads of the two Poplars, & disturbs the murmur of the moonlight Greta, that in almost a direct Line from the moon to me is all silver—Motion and Wrinkle & Light—& under the arch of the Bridge a wave ever & anon leaps up in Light—& the evergreens are bright under my window. The Moon now hangs midway over Cowdale Halse—in a line, & resting on each of the divergent Legs of its Triangle a fish-head-shaped Cloud—the whole area of the Triangle blue Sky—but above the Cloud, & in

---

[1] MS Note-Book No. 21. Add. MSS 47518, ff. 82v–83.

[2] MS Note-Book No. 16. Add. MSS 47513, f. 28v. "Passively" is not quite certain.

[3] *AP*, p. 27. MS Note-Book No. 8 (Add. MSS 47505, f. 49) reads "Repose after agitation Pool under waterfalls, made by the waterfall Thurs Jan 20 left Keswick" in scrawled, and even agitated, pencil writing. See also below, p. 56 *n*.

the interspace between it and the Moon little cloudlets, scarcely larger than large Stars.—Wrinkles,—long [roundish] [1] floating Braids of Hair floating & making its single Hairs distinguishable, as it wantons on some regular Breeze/ black smooth Space of Shade—silver mirror/ gleaming of moonlight Reeds beyond—as the moon sets the water from Silver becomes a rich yellow.—Sadly do I need to have my Imagination enriched with appropriate Images for Shapes./ Read Architecture, & Ichthyology.[2]

We can best be helped to an understanding of this by a few sentences from one of the finest of all his letters, written to Sotheby on 10 September 1802: he has just been discussing some of Bowles's later poems:

Never to see or describe any interesting appearance in nature without connecting it, by dim analogies, with the moral world proves faintness of impression. Nature has her proper interest, and he will know what it is who believes and feels that everything has a life of its own, and that we are all *One Life*. A poet's heart and intellect should be *combined*, intimately combined and unified with the great appearances of nature, and not merely held in solution and loose mixture with them, in the shape of formal similes.[3]

A full commentary on those sentences would go far into Coleridge's heart; from all it has to offer we must now be content with selecting three points: that the *strength of impression* of external nature on the mind is the essential starting-point; that nature has her own *proper* interest irrespective of a secondary act of application to moralised human life; and that this proper interest derives from the dual fact that everything (including a human being), while having its own life, yet shares in the common life of all.

He recurs again and again to the vitality of changing shapes which he realises in his own fertile imagery and shifting rhythms. This is a note of 27 November 1799:

Soon after this I saw Starlings in vast Flights, borne along like smoke, mist—like a body unindued with voluntary

---

[1] "Roundish" rather doubtful.

[2] MS Note-Book No. 21. Add. MSS 47518, f. 73.

[3] *L*, I, 403-4.

Power—now it shaped itself into a circular area, inclined—
now they formed a Square—now a Globe—now from [a]
complete orb into an Ellipse—then oblongated into a Balloon
with the Car suspended, now a concave Semicircle; still
expanding, or contracting, thinning or condensing, now
glimmering and shivering, now thickening, deepening, black-
ening! [1]

The changes of shape and light and movement are all
realised at once; and it is in the very movement of the
style that we see the attunement of the personality to the
birds.

One of the most beautifully developed short descriptions in all Coleridge's writing is this, written about one
small spot in the Tees at Barnard Castle, where the
river runs fast and shallow over rocks:

The *white rose* of Eddy-foam, where the stream ran into a
scooped or scolloped hollow of the Rock in it's channel—this
Shape, an exact white rose, was for ever overpowered by the
Stream rushing down in upon it, and still obstinate in resurrection it spread up into the Scollop, by fits & starts, *blossoming*
in a moment into a full Flower.[2]

The perfect fitness of this flower-image, to the combination of the shape itself with its repeated disappearance
and reappearance, is brought about by the use of the
verb "blossoming" for each recurrence. And the phrase
"obstinate in resurrection" could not be bettered to
convey the strength behind each surprising, fresh,
renewal. We are presented at once with the beauty of a
form and with the vitality of nature by which the form
persists through the very force of the matter which both
destroys and creates it. He writes, after describing a
waterfall at length to Sara Hutchinson:

What a sight it is to look down on such a Cataract! The
wheels, that circumvolve in it, the leaping up and plunging
forward of that infinity of Pearls and Glass Bulbs, the continual

---

[1] Quoted in *Note-Books and Papers of Gerard Manley Hopkins*, ed. H.
House (1937), p. 401 from MS Note-Book No. 21. Add. MSS 47518,
f. 56v. Text revised.

[2] MS Note-Book No. 21. Add. MSS 47518, f. 56.

change of the *Matter*, the perpetual *Sameness* of the *Form*—it is an awful Image and Shadow of God and the World.[1]

Immediately following on the description of the rose of eddy-foam in the Tees, on the same page, after a couple of dashes, comes this:

Hung over the Bridge, & musing considering how much of this Scene of endless variety in Identity was Nature's—how much the living organ's! What would it be if I had the eyes of a fly!—What if the blunt eye of a Brobdignag!—[2]

[1] *Inquiring Spirit*, ed. Coburn, p. 241. Among "the instances of the proverb 'Extremes Meet'" comes: "In the foam-islands in a fiercely boiling pool, at the bottom of a waterfall, there is sameness from infinite change" (*AP*, p. 52).

[2] See below, pp. 75–6.

CHAPTER III

THE PROBLEM OF POETIC STYLE

In view of what in fact he achieved, Coleridge was quite unbelievably modest about his own poems; and the modesty was of a curious kind, sometimes rather humble and over-elaborate, sometimes apparently quite candid, because he did not see the merits that others have found since. He was very willing to quote extracts from his own poems in the course of his argument in prose works and in conversation; but this is rather a different matter, for it is only likely that he should think his own poems had said *something* that had not been said quite so appositely anywhere else. But in some instances there was an almost self-destructive honesty and candour. Why was it necessary, for instance, to publish "Kubla Khan" for the first time only in 1816, so many years after it was written? And to publish it then with the enormous preface? Of course, we are glad to have the preface now. But why was it necessary at the very first appearance to give that long account of the poem's genesis, itself including ten distracting lines of another of his own poems, all on the supposition that "Kubla Khan" was published "rather as a psychological curiosity, than on the ground of any supposed *poetic* merits"?

If it had been slipped in, say, to the small volume of 1803, as a matter of course, with no preface or explanation, how different its history might have been! If nobody had ever heard about the dream or the anodyne or the "person on business from Porlock", what might "Kubla Khan" not have done to critics? The answer to that question—or some groping towards an answer— belongs to Chapter V.

If we look at the contents of that volume of 1803 it is

astonishing to discover what isn't there, in view of what we know to have been written at that time. No "Ancient Mariner", no "Kubla Khan", no "Christabel", no "Frost at Midnight", no "Lime-Tree Bower", no "Dejection": not even "France: an Ode" is there, even though it had been printed in *The Morning Post*. We can perhaps understand that the *Lyrical Ballads* poems should not have been reprinted, because they belonged to another context; and "Christabel" was still clouded by a hope of completion. But why all these other omissions? Why *not* make a proper collected edition in 1803? Why not make *Sybilline Leaves* more complete in 1817? There was no attempt at "collecting" till 1828, when he was fifty-six.

It is useless to talk of a mistaken policy of publication. There was no policy. Coleridge dreaded publication; it harassed him and threw him out. He wrote to Jeffrey in November 1808, in one of those gloriously prolonged figures of speech, of which he was such a master:

Hitherto, I have layed my Eggs with Ostrich Carelessness and Ostrich Oblivion—the greater part indeed have been crushed under foot; but some have crawled into light to furnish Feathers for other men's Caps, and not a few to plume the shafts of the Quivers of my Calumniators.[1]

This was written at the time when he was first hopefully planning *The Friend*, the worst conceived and worst mismanaged of all mismanaged publications; and the words were repeated, with few changes, and justifiable pride, in a letter to Tom Poole on 4 December.[2]

In proportion as he discovered his own genius to himself he seems to have become more nervous of trying to assess it: even in the Note-Books, pathetically at one time called "my sole confidants", there is no reference to having written "Frost at Midnight" or "The Ancient Mariner" or "Kubla Khan"; and even though he regrets

[1] To Francis Jeffrey, 10 Nov 1808; *UL*, I, 431. This image appears first in Note-Book No. 21 in 1803: then in a letter to Poole, 14 Oct 1803; *UL*, I, 289: it was made public in *BL*, I, 32.
[2] *UL*, I, 433.

so often the loss of the "shaping spirit of imagination", he never commits himself to confessing what he deeply believed it best had shaped. He held on, with revisions and fresh editions, to the little corpus of his pre-Wordsworth poems, in a cherishing, muted way, long after they had been superseded. In one or two instances, such as "The Eolian Harp", he made quite late changes which enormously improved them. But when he came to sum up this early work in the *Biographia* he cheerfully and fully discussed its faults with a perspicuity we can build upon.

He found these charges made against the poems—obscurity, "a general turgidness of diction, and a profusion of new coined double epithets". About the obscurity, he said:

... my mind was not then sufficiently disciplined to receive the authority of others, as a substitute for my own conviction. Satisfied that the thoughts, such as they were, could not have been expressed otherwise, or at least more perspicuously, I forgot to enquire, whether the thoughts themselves did not demand a degree of attention unsuitable to the nature and objects of poetry. This remark however applies chiefly, though not exclusively, to the *Religious Musings*.[1]

After then stating, perhaps with some slight exaggeration, that he later "pruned the double epithets with no sparing hand" and used his "best efforts to tame the swell and glitter both of thought and diction",[2] he continues:

My judgement was stronger, than were my powers of realizing its dictates; and the faults of my language, though indeed partly owing to a wrong choice of subjects, and the desire of giving a poetic colouring to abstract and metaphysical truths, in which a new world then seemed to open upon me, did yet, in part likewise, originate in unfeigned diffidence of my own comparative talent.[3]

Behind the more rich and interesting of these very early poems—I mean the "Religious Musings", some of the sonnets, the "Ode to the Departing Year", "Reflections

[1] *BL*, I, 2–3.
[2] These phrases first appear in the Preface to the Second Edition of *Poems*, 1797.   [3] *BL*, I, p. 3.

on having left a Place of Retirement", and "The Destiny of Nations" (though that was not brought together in its present form till 1817, and even then might well have been left dismembered, for there never was a poem with less superficial unity)—there is an underlying impulse towards the unification of two kinds of subject in one poetic whole. His later opinion, that the choice of subjects was "wrong", was made from a quite different point of view from that which was his in the mid-nineties. For at that time the subjects were to him necessities, if he was to have any significant relation at all to the life of his age. The two main subjects with which he was concerned were philosophical religion and politics; and these early poems should be regarded as attempts to unify the modes of apprehending those two things. When we come upon those three extra-ordinary lines towards the end of the "Reflections"

> I therefore go, and join head, heart, and hand,
> Active and firm, to fight the bloodless fight
> Of Science, Freedom, and the Truth in Christ [1]

we may smile in view of our knowledge of his later history, but we shall never understand his later history unless we ponder on them carefully.

In the mid-nineties Coleridge and Wordsworth, along with many other young men, some of whom were their friends, faced a similar set of problems, though they approached the solution of them differently. Both were caught up in the political crisis and in the moral and emotional crisis which developed from it. Pantisocracy should not be treated too lightly as just a typical product of late eighteenth-century sentimental Utopianism; of course it was that; the formal details of the scheme were ridiculous enough; Coleridge's style in writing of it was often that of a "Godwin Methodist"—"SHAD GOES WITH US. HE IS MY BROTHER! . . . Make Edith my sister. . . . She must . . . be more emphatically my sister".[2]

---

[1] ll. 60–2; *PW*, I, 108.

[2] To Southey, 18 Sep 1794; *L*, I, 82. Shad was the Southey family servant.

Such factitious affection suggests an uneasy enough basis for the positive side of the scheme: but negatively it grew from a depth of terrible experience. Behind it lay a genuine agony of disappointment and shame at the contemporary condition of England; a dilemma of morals and of patriotic emotion. In his horror at the beginning of war in February 1793, Wordsworth was not alone:

> Not in my single self alone I found,
> But in the minds of all ingenuous Youth,
> Change and subversion from this hour. No shock
> Given to my moral nature had I known
> Down to that very moment.[1]

He exulted "when Englishmen by thousands were o'er-thrown". In church, when prayers or praises were offered for victory, he alone prayed in the opposite sense, and fed on the vengeance to come. So, too, Coleridge had been plunged into this "conflict of sensations without name" and he described it in "France: an Ode":

> Unawed I sang, amid a slavish band:
> And when to whelm the disenchanted nation,
> Like fiends embattled by a wizard's wand,
>   The Monarchs marched in evil day,
>   And Britain joined the dire array;
> Though dear her shores and circling ocean,
> Though many friendships, many youthful loves
>   Had swoln the patriot emotion
> And flung a magic light o'er all her hills and groves;
> Yet still my voice, unaltered, sang defeat
>   To all that braved the tyrant-quelling lance,
> And shame too long delayed and vain retreat!
> For ne'er, O Liberty! with partial aim
> I dimmed thy light or damped thy holy flame;
>   But blessed the paeans of delivered France,
> And hung my head and wept at Britain's name.[2]

Coleridge too had been thrown "out of the pale of love".

The double-sidedness of the situation is clearly present within the "Pantisocracy" sonnet of 1794. The octet touches on the "shame and anguish of the evil day"

---

[1] *Prelude* (1805–6), X, 232 ff.   [2] st. ii, ll. 27–42; *PW*, I, 245.

which must be forgotten before the achievement of Utopian calm; and in the sestet the pantisocratic hope is presented altogether as the thankful relief of one waking from a nightmare:

> Eyes that have ach'd with Sorrow! Ye shall weep
> Tears of doubt-mingled joy, like theirs who start
> From Precipices of distemper'd sleep,
> On which the fierce-eyed Fiends their revels keep,
> And see the rising Sun, and feel it dart
> New rays of pleasance trembling to the heart.[1]

Those "Precipices of distemper'd sleep" stand even rhythmically in relief above their context. Nor are they merely personal to one who knew the feverish dreams of illness and the miseries of being a Trooper of Dragoons; they express the anguish of the patriotic dilemma, after a year of war, at the time of the government panic and the State Trials. The "Monody on the Death of Chatterton", in the version printed in 1796, ends with the author imagined on the banks of the Susquehannah, musing on the "sore ills" he had left behind.[2] Even if the second Pantisocracy sonnet is not by Coleridge himself, yet it shows even more clearly among his contemporaries the mood from which the plans for emigration sprang:

> Whilst pale Anxiety, corrosive Care,
> The tear of Woe, the gloom of sad Despair,
>   And deepen'd Anguish generous bosoms rend;—
> Whilst patriot souls their country's fate lament;
> Whilst mad with rage demoniac, foul intent,
>   Embattled legions Despots vainly send
> To arrest the immortal mind's expanding ray
>   Of everlasting Truth;—I other climes
> . . . .
> With mental eye exulting now explore . . .[3]

---

[1] *PW*, I, 69 and p. 68, where the authorship is discussed: cf. *L*, I, 83, 109–10. Writing to Southey, 11 Dec 1794, Coleridge said: "Of the sonnet, 'No more the visionary soul shall dwell', I wrote the whole but the second and third lines"; these were probably by Favell. There is little reason to doubt Coleridge's authorship of the six lines quoted above.

[2] *PW*, I, 130–1 and *n*.   [3] *ibid.*, 69 and *n*.

Wordsworth and Coleridge faced a similar set of problems. Neither of them had made any formal decision to be "poets", or at least to be poets only or mainly. They felt primarily the need for action. In that wonderful part of *The Prelude* when Wordsworth returns to Paris after the September Massacres and ponders in his garret on what it all implies, he wonders whether he himself may not be called on to become a political leader.

But for him, and for Coleridge too, the only available kind of action (such schemes as Pantisocracy apart) was some sort of writing or talk, in fact the writing of propaganda.[1] And the literary problem then becomes the problem of what is the most effective form of literary propaganda. Coleridge tried political sermons; Wordsworth wrote a political pamphlet which (with less courage) he never published. But both inevitably found themselves involved in experiments in the use of poetry for propaganda purposes. Wordsworth embarked on the various writings and re-writings of what was called his Salisbury Plain Poem, which ended up as "Guilt and Sorrow"—of which "The Female Vagrant" formed a part—and it was in this poem that Coleridge first recognised the emergence of Wordsworth's new style: "There was here no mark of strained thought, or forced diction, no crowd or turbulence of imagery." [2] But both in this dilemma turned to Milton, as the great prototype of the poet who had been politician and man of literary action too. It is notable in *The Prelude* how, when Wordsworth in later memory is recalling his own contemplation of political action, the verse takes its whole character from Miltonic rhythms and echoes. With Coleridge the case is just as plain. He wrote to Tom Poole in a relaxed mood in December 1796: "My poetic vanity and my political *furor* have been exhaled; and I would rather be an expert self-maintaining gardener

[1] cf. *L*, I, 194, To Thelwall, 17 Dec 1796: "I am not *fit* for *public* life; yet the light shall stream to a far distance from my cottage window."

[2] *BL*, I, 58.

than a Milton, if I could not unite both." [1] The following lines from "Religious Musings" are a positive pastiche of Milton:

> For the Great
> Invisible (by symbols only seen)
> With a peculiar and surpassing light
> Shines from the visage of the oppressed good man,
> When heedless of himself the scourgéd saint
> Mourns for the oppressor. Fair the vernal mead,
> Fair the high grove, the sea, the sun, the stars;
> True impress each of their creating Sire!
> Yet nor high grove, nor many-colour'd mead,
> Nor the green ocean with his thousand isles,
> Nor the starred azure, nor the sovran sun,
> E'er with such majesty of portraiture
> Imaged the supreme beauty uncreate,
> As thou, meek Saviour! [2]

"Religious Musings" in its first form was written on Christmas Eve 1794; and in that Miltonic mood it was no accident that the first of the "Sonnets on Eminent Characters" in *The Morning Chronicle* in December 1794 should have been addressed to Erskine; for he was then at the height of his extraordinary success and popularity as counsel for the defence in the political prosecutions instituted, in something like a panic, by the Government. In 1792 Erskine had failed to get an acquittal for Tom Paine, but his closing speech with its eulogy of Harrington and its final splendid appeal to Milton [3]—a pointed and classic example of the many links between the liberal Whigs at the end of the eighteenth century and the Republicans of the seventeenth—had marked him as the ideal advocate to meet the "thunder of authority". In May 1793, John Frost

---

[1] *L*, I, 192.

[2] ll. 9–22; *PW*, I, 109–10. The imitation of *Paradise Lost*, IV, 641–56 was not part of the published version of 1796, but first appears in the MS part of the Potts copy of *Poems*, 1796, whence it is printed in *Coleridge's Poems*, A Facsimile Reproduction of the Proofs and MSS of some of the Poems, ed. J. Dykes Campbell and W. Hale White (1899), p. 8. It thus dates between 16 April 1796 and May 1797: see *PW*, II, 1135 and 1146.

[3] T. B. and T. J. Howell, *State Trials*, XXII (1817), 410–72.

was convicted in spite of Erskine's defence;[1] but in December he got an acquittal for Perry and Gray, the proprietors of *The Morning Chronicle*;[2] in April 1794 he got a verdict of not-guilty for Walker[3] on a charge of a conspiracy to overthrow the Government; in October 1794 he spoke continuously for seven hours, to win the acquittal of Hardy; then followed the acquittal of Horne Tooke in November.[4] Erskine's eloquence and courage seemed to belong to the last age of heroic English politics. Portraits and busts and tokens with his face on them were sold all over the country ; and among this spate of various tributes came Coleridge's sonnet, in tune with Erskine in its deliberate Miltonic echoes: at Freedom's altar

> . . . dreadless thou didst stand
> (Thy censer glowing with the hallow'd flame)
> A hireless Priest before the insulted shrine,
> And at her altar pour the stream divine
> Of unmatch'd eloquence.[5]

Miltonic reminiscences occur all through that series of sonnets in December 1794 and January 1795. Pitt, attacked by Sheridan,

> Writhes inly from the bosom-probing glance
> The Apostate by the brainless rout ador'd,
> As erst that elder Fiend beneath great Michael's sword.[6]

and Earl Stanhope, in the later-cancelled sonnet,

> . . . aye unterrify'd
> Pourest thine Abdiel warnings on the train
> That sit complotting with rebellious pride[7]

against the liberty of France.

This Miltonising is not a mere matter of poetical

[1] T. B. and T. J. Howell, *State Trials*, XXII (1817), 488–519.
[2] *ibid.*, 995–1019.   [3] *State Trials*, XXIII, 1055–1166.
[4] *State Trials*, XXIV, 877–1111; XXV, 257–497.
[5] *PW*, I, 79–80; Coleridge wrote to Southey, 11 Dec 1794: "My sonnets to eminent contemporaries are among the better things I have written. That to Erskine is a bad specimen" (*L*, I, 112).
[6] "To Richard Brinsley Sheridan, Esq.", ll. 12–14; *PW*, I, 88.
[7] *PW*, I, 89; for Coleridge's later opinion and account of this sonnet, see letter to Miss Cruikshanks, in Joseph Cottle, *Reminiscences* (1847), p. 111.

echoes, such as might be found at any time through the eighteenth century; it is part of a conscious political act. But for Coleridge at all stages of development politics and religion were inseparable—the tri-form praise of Priestley was that he was "patriot, saint, and sage"—and in an age when the Church and King party appealed to the principle that the Christian religion was "part and parcel of the Common Law of England", Milton became the symbolic figure of a double opposition.

In poetry too Milton became the justification for Coleridge's attempts to combine political and philosophically religious themes. The way in which he attempted this synthesis appears perhaps most clearly in the first part of "The Destiny of Nations":

> Such symphony requires best instrument.
> Seize, then, my soul! from Freedom's trophied dome
> The Harp which hangeth high between the Shields
> Of Brutus and Leonidas! With that
> Strong music, that soliciting spell, force back
> Man's free and stirring spirit that lies entranced.
> For what is Freedom, but the unfettered use
> Of all the powers which God for use had given?
> But chiefly this, him First, him Last to view
> Through meaner powers and secondary things
> Effulgent, as through clouds that veil his blaze.
> For all that meets the bodily sense I deem
> Symbolical, one mighty alphabet
> For infant minds; and we in this low world
> Placed with our backs to bright Reality,
> That we may learn with young unwounded ken
> The substance from its shadow. Infinite Love,
> Whose latence is the plenitude of All,
> Thou with retracted beams, and self-eclipse
> Veiling, revealest thine eternal Sun.[1]

These lines are full of Miltonic echoes; and in them political freedom is identical with the intellectual freedom to be an enthusiastic Platonist.

In one sense the shadow of *Paradise Lost* hung over all Coleridge's life. It gave him the last great example in English of a poem which had unified all the diverse

[1] ll. 7–26; *PW*, I, 132.

kinds of human knowledge. He thought of himself as perhaps once more achieving a seventeenth-century range and inclusiveness; and there is little doubt that, at least intermittently, he modelled himself on Milton, in ordering his reading with the deliberate intention of writing a great philosophical poem. And much of the material which appeared almost by chance in "The Ancient Mariner" had been collected with that purpose in view.

He wrote to Cottle in 1796:

> The story of Milton might be told in two pages. It is this which distinguishes an epic poem from a romance in metre. Observe the march of Milton; his severe application; his laborious polish; his deep metaphysical researches; his prayer to God before he began his great work; all that could lift and swell his intellect became his daily food.
>
> I should not think of devoting less than twenty years to an epic poem. Ten years to collect materials and warm my mind with universal science. I would be a tolerable mathematician. I would thoroughly understand Mechanics; Hydrostatics; Optics, and Astronomy; Botany; Metallurgy; Fossilism; Chemistry; Geology; Anatomy; Medicine; then the mind of man; then the minds of men, in all Travels, Voyages and Histories. So I would spend ten years; the next five in the composition of the poem, and the last five in the correction of it. So would I write, haply not unhearing of that divine and nightly-whispering voice, which speaks to mighty minds, of predestined garlands, starry and unwithering.[1]

We know that Coleridge himself was thwarted in these great aims partly by ill-health and unhappiness; but we also know the deep disappointment he expressed when Wordsworth failed to produce the great "philosophical" poem he had hoped to see. Coleridge did not fail alone. Shelley and, later, T. L. Beddoes were haunted by the possibility of such a synthesis between poetry and the various sciences. But we have to ask whether the increasing specialisation and range, the elaboration of detailed method, in the sciences, did not, even during Coleridge's middle life, make impossible the imaginative

---

[1] Joseph Cottle, *Reminiscences* (1847), p. 103.

treatment of the whole field of human knowledge. His own friends (like the elder Beddoes and Humphry Davy) or his heroes (like Priestley) not only stimulated his hope, but made its achievement more unlikely, as their work and that of their successors progressed.

Apart from questions of subject, the other problem that both Wordsworth and Coleridge had to face was—what was to be the poetic idiom of verse propaganda? We must leave aside their attempts at more conventional and personal political satire, in favour of the poems which were meant to guide their readers through their emotions towards the opinions proposed. A very great deal of political verse was being written at the time; they were compassed round with various samples and precedents of style. There were, for instance, the Gray-like Ode precedents and the Darwin-like periphrastic precedents. And to understand not only the problems of finding a political style, but also the hatred of "gawdy and inane phraseology" in the declared policy of *Lyrical Ballads*, it is helpful to look at examples of these.

The first example is from the *Secular Ode in Commemoration of the Glorious Revolution*, by W. Mason, M.A., London, 1788. Stanza v reads thus, the "she" of these lines being the Goddess Freedom:

> Still louder lift the Soul-expanding strain,
> >   Ye future years! while, from her starry throne,
> Again she comes to magnify her reign,
> >   And make the world her own.
> >   Her fire e'en France presumes to feel,
> >   And half unsheathes the patriot steel,
> >   >   Enough the monarch to dismay,
> >   Who'er, with rebel pride, withdraws
> >   His own allegiance from the laws
> That guard the people's rights, that rein the sovereign's
> >   >   >   >   >   sway.[1]

Such a poem as this is interesting for a number of different reasons in describing the political atmosphere

[1] Original text, identical (apart from slight changes of capitalisation and punctuation) with that in *The Works of William Mason M.A.*, in Four Volumes (1811), I, 73.

in which Wordsworth and Coleridge grew up; it shows, for instance, the importance of the Centenary of the 1688 Revolution as a link between the American War of Independence and the French Revolution; it shows how leftish Whigs were casting sympathetic eyes towards events in France even before the dramatic moment of the fall of the Bastille; but I quote it now to illustrate the current convention of singing political odes, and how the imagery and machinery of the exalted love of Freedom—"the starry throne", "the patriot steel" and so on—could be called on to enforce even the Whig interpretation of the English Constitution. Coleridge used and assimilated the Ode style and made it his own. He gave it a vigour and directness for propagandist purposes. In this kind "France: an Ode" is one of the best achievements of the whole political poetry of that period.

The next example is from *The Art of War* by Joseph Fawcett. Fawcett was known to Wordsworth and provided the basis of the character of the Solitary in *The Excursion*. *The Art of War* is a didactic pacifist propaganda poem in blank verse published by J. Johnson in 1795: the following lines treat the old opposition between ploughshares and swords, pruning-hooks and spears:

> See all Nature's gifts,
> Given but for good, made instruments of ill!
> From the dug earth educ'd, behold that ore,
> Of highest worth, in richest plenty giv'n,
> His bounty such who stock'd the ball He built,
> Of friendly edge susceptive, form'd to serve,
> With smooth incision, useful Art's fair ends,—
> See its fine point employ'd, ah! not to fetch
> Forth from the furrow'd earth the golden bread;
> Call copious Plenty o'er her vales to laugh;
> Or prune with œconomic cut away
> Her wasteful growth;—but, amputation foul!
> Lop human life, and with an impious edge
> With purple dropping, plough the flesh of man! [1]

When Fawcett wishes to describe the burning of the crops in a campaign, he writes: "beauteous Ceres to a

[1] *The Art of War. A Poem* (1795), p. 10.

cinder change". A musket is, of course, "the tube of death", in the same convention as the familiar "thundering tube" which the aged angler heard in Wordsworth's *Descriptive Sketches*.[1] Coleridge's own reform in his poetic diction and idiom can be seen best as a moving away from Fawcett and from Miltonising towards Cowperising. Cowper was his route to his own kinds of achieved simplicity. The achievement was not easy: even as late as January 1798, discussing the ballad song in Lewis's *Castle-Spectre*, he could write:

The simplicity and naturalness is his own, and not imitated; for it is made to subsist in congruity with a language perfectly modern, the language of his own times, in the same way that the language of the writer of "Sir Cauline" was the language of *his* times. This, I think, a rare merit: at least, I find, *I* cannot attain this innocent nakedness, except by *assumption*. I resemble the Duchess of Kingston, who masqueraded in the character of "Eve before the Fall", in flesh-coloured Silk.[2]

This points along two directions of Coleridge's development. The mention of "Sir Cauline" at once suggests "The Ancient Mariner", a genuine imaginative achievement in a language not "perfectly modern", a triumph of assumption. But the wish to be simple in a modern idiom has its fulfilment in the group of poems of which the best known are "The Nightingale", "This Lime-Tree Bower my Prison", "The Eolian Harp" and "Frost at Midnight". For in these poems, apart from the occasional awkward apostrophisings and double negatives and a residue of Miltonisms, Coleridge ceases to be a poet who "echoes the conceit", ceases to be a

> Poet who hath been building up the rhyme
> When he had better far have stretched his limbs
> Beside a brook in mossy forest-dell,
> By sun or moon-light, to the influxes
> Of shapes and sounds and shifting elements
> Surrendering his whole spirit, of his song
> And of his fame forgetful![3]

---

[1] l. 66, 1793; the phrase was kept in the final version, l. 61.
[2] Letter to Wordsworth, Jan 1798; *L*, I, 237.
[3] "The Nightingale", ll. 23–30; *PW*, I, 265.

This group of poems belongs, most obviously, in kind, with Wordsworth's "Tintern Abbey". The kind is a peculiar one, which no poets before Wordsworth and Coleridge, I think, had quite hit upon or found the internal need to devise. A clue to its nature is given in the subtitle to "The Nightingale", as that was first published in *Lyrical Ballads*; it is there called "The Nightingale, a Conversational Poem".[1] A similar idea was expressed in the original sub-title of the poem now called "Reflections on having left a place of Retirement"; it was called "Reflections on entering into active life. A Poem which affects not to be Poetry"; and a motto was prefixed in 1797 from Horace (*Satires*, I, 4, 42): "Sermoni propriora"—that is, "more fitted for talk or prose", the language of ordinary life.[2] The blank verse poems of this group are all avowedly autobiographical. Their type of verse is best to be understood by comparing it with Cowper's.

The importance of Cowper to the poetic environment in which Coleridge grew up is perhaps greater and more marked than that of Collins,[3] and in the long run certainly greater than that of Bowles.[4] The long poem to be called "The Brook" which Coleridge was planning in 1797 was to be in the manner of Cowper's *Task*; and on Hazlitt's famous visit to Nether Stowey in the spring of 1798 Coleridge "spoke of Cowper as the best modern poet", in the same conversation as he "spoke

---

[1] *PW*, I, 264: it was later called "A Conversation Poem".

[2] *ibid.*, 106.

[3] The highest peak of admiration for Collins appears in the letter to Thelwall of December 1796: "Now Collins's "Ode on the Poetical Character,"—that part of it, I should say, beginning with "The band (as faery legends say) Was wove on that creating day,"—has inspired and whirled *me* along with greater agitations of enthusiasm than any the most *impassioned* scene in Schiller or Shakespeare...." (*L*, I, 196–7). Coleridge's "growing out of" Collins's Odes provides part of the context of the famous phrase about poetry "not perfectly understood" (see above pp. 29–30 and *n*.). Collins's "Ode on the Passions" unmistakably provided a phrase and two words in "Kubla Khan" (see Lowes, pp. 399–400).

[4] *BL*, I, 8–9.

with contempt of Gray".[1] But the phrase of Coleridge which best expresses what he found is "the divine chit-chat of Cowper";[2] and the most striking likeness and contrast between them is in a comparison of Coleridge's "Frost at Midnight" with a section of *The Task*, Book IV.[3]

"The Brook" was never written. The account in the *Biographia* mentions "studies" which were made for it; and the suspicions of local residents and the Government spy are now notorious.[4] But in the Gutch Memorandum Book are some notes which must almost certainly be some of the "studies" for the poem:

> The brook runs over Sea-weeds.—
> Sabbath day—from the Miller's mossy wheel the
>   waterdrops dripp'd leisurely—
>   on the broad mountaintop
> The neighing wild-colt races with the wind
> O'er fern and heath-flowers—
>   A long deep Lane
> So over shadowed, it might seem one bower —
> The damp Clay banks were furr'd with mouldy moss
>   Broad-breasted Pollards with broad-branching
>   head.[5]

Cowper was the great current example of a poet using blank verse, freely, easily, for personal purposes, as the metre of conversational matter and a conversational vocabulary.

Most of *The Task* is either autobiographical or descriptive; further, the autobiographical elements and the descriptive elements are linked: the things described are mostly described because they have given Cowper pleasure, and the pleasure he takes in them is itself

[1] "My First Acquantance with Poets", Centenary Edition, ed. P. P. Howe (1933), XVII, 120–1; cf. P. P. Howe, *Life of William Hazlitt*, Penguin edn., p. 68.

[2] *L*, I, 197, and *n. ad loc.*

[3] See below, pp. 78–9.

[4] *BL*, I, 129. See also A. J. Eagleston, "Wordsworth, Coleridge, and the Spy", *Coleridge, Studies by Several Hands*, ed. E. Blunden and E. L. Griggs (1934), pp. 73–87.

[5] As quoted by Lowes, p. 522, *n.* 53.

described, with varying moods and phases. In Book I, for instance, where he is describing Painting and Nature, he says that Painting can please only "the eye", whereas "sweet Nature" pleases "every sense".

> The air salubrious of her lofty hills,
> The cheering fragrance of her dewy vales,
> And music of her woods—no works of man
> May rival these; these all bespeak a pow'r
> Peculiar, and exclusively her own.[1]

Cowper here leads up to the boundary of Coleridge; the fact is that Cowper's treatment of such pleasure is shallow and in the last resort unimportant; such verse has not got "high seriousness"; it is "chit-chat"; just as there is little thought about the quality and implications of the pleasure, so the verse has none of the variety and vigour such thought can give.

In the Conversation poems Coleridge is carrying on where Cowper left off. The autobiographical element is given deeper psychological analysis, and the thought about it carries over into what is properly metaphysical poetry. The informal method is kept; but everything has greater import; the imagery leaves Cowper's direct statement; the descriptive passages are more intricately and closely knit to their psychological effects; the description is more minute, delicate and various in correspondence with the more minute and various states of mind on which it bears. Above all, the language of some of the poems, particularly "Frost at Midnight", has the verbal concentration on which great poetry always depends, and Cowper so obviously nearly always lacks.

The earliest poem which at all fully expresses the attunement of the human spirit to nature is "The Eolian Harp", written in its first version in 1795. The image of the Eolian Harp with the wind making music on its strings occurs in "The Nightingale" and by implication in "Fears in Solitude" where in the young man (as on its strings) "many feelings, many thoughts" are

[1] "The Sofa", rather over half-way through.

unified into a *harmony* of "meditative joy".[1] In "Dejection: an Ode", as we shall see later, it occurs in an important way again.

"The Eolian Harp" opens with Coleridge sitting with Sara, soon to be his wife, beside their cottage, where they watch

> the clouds, that late were rich with light,
> Slow saddening round, and mark the star of eve
> Serenely brilliant (such should Wisdom be)
> Shine opposite! How exquisite the scents
> Snatch'd from yon bean-field! and the world *so* hush'd!
> The stilly murmur of the distant Sea
> Tells us of silence.
>   And that simplest Lute,
> Placed length-ways in the clasping casement, hark!
> How by the desultory breeze caress'd,
> Like some coy maid half yielding to her lover,
> It pours such sweet upbraiding, as must needs
> Tempt to repeat the wrong! And now, its strings
> Boldlier swept, the long sequacious notes
> Over delicious surges sink and rise,
> Such a soft floating witchery of sound
> As twilight Elfins make, when they at eve
> Voyage on gentle gales from Fairy-Land,
> Where Melodies round honey-dropping flowers,
> Footless and wild, like birds of Paradise,
> Nor pause, nor perch, hovering on untam'd wing![2]

The clouds and light show powers of detailed description beginning to develop before the close association with the Wordsworths; and the final line, about the birds of Paradise, shows the fine rhythmical sensitivity to subtle and various kinds of movement which appears, for instance, in the prose description of the starlings,[3] or in the lines about the source of the river in "Kubla Khan".

[1] ll. 22–3; *PW*, I, 257.

[2] ll. 6–25 of the *textus receptus* of 1834; *PW*, I, 100–101; drafts dated 1795 and 1797 are given, from the Cottle MSS at Rugby School, in *PW*, II, 1021–2. ll. 6–8½ are, apart from punctuation and orthography, identical in all three versions; ll. 10–11½ are identical except that both Cottle MSS read "far-off" for "distant".

[3] See above, pp. 54–5.

74

It is important to realise that the beautiful lines 26–33 formed no part of the original poem. They appear in almost exactly this form for the first time in the Errata to *Sibylline Leaves*, 1817.

> O! the one Life within us and abroad,
> Which meets all motion and becomes its soul,
> A light in sound, a sound-like power in light,
> Rhythm in all thought, and joyance every where —
> Methinks, it should have been impossible
> Not to love all things in a world so fill'd;
> Where the breeze warbles, and the mute still air
> Is Music slumbering on her instrument.

These lines are one of Coleridge's mature expressions in verse of the idea developed in the letter to Sotheby of September 1802, the idea that "everything has a life of its own, and that we are all *One Life*". They do not in themselves seem to demand, discuss or reject a choice between a "realist" and a "projectionist" view of nature;[1] they seem rather a statement of a fundamental undivided attunement, not only of the human mind to external nature but also of elements of external nature to each other. The line "a light in sound, a sound-like power in light", would, as psychologically relevant to the human mind, imply coenaesthesia; but that is not the side of the matter that is here being stressed. What *is* being stressed is that in such moments of "joyance" we become acutely aware that the nature we know appears exactly as it does in its bearings of part to part within itself, and in its bearings towards us, because of a fundamental attunement between us and it. Leaning over the Barnard Castle bridge Coleridge asked himself what it would all be like if he had the eyes of a fly or the eye of a Brobdignag.[2] That is what we can never know. The physical constitution we have fits us to know just the nature we do know, and precludes us from knowing any other. At certain moments of concentration and happiness we become acutely aware of this essential

---

[1] See Richards, Ch. vii, esp. pp. 144–9.
[2] See above, p. 56.

interaction, through a sympathy by which movement in nature harmonises with rhythms in ourselves.

These lines link to the music of the wind-harp in quite a different way from the lines (44–8) which did form part of the poem as published in 1796 [1]—

> And what if all of animated nature
> Be but organic Harps diversely fram'd,
> That tremble into thought, as o'er them sweeps
> Plastic and vast, one intellectual breeze,
> At once the Soul of each, and God of all?

These lines (44–8) are far less closely connected than lines 26–33 to modes of perception through the senses; they seem much more a broad Neo-Platonist theological speculation about the world in general, and much less a poetic statement of personal experience. The late grafting on of lines 26–33, which follow admirably from the beginning, has immensely improved the poem up to that point; but it has completely thrown out its balance as a whole, and virtually made nonsense of the unaltered ending. In the accepted version lines 49–64, at the end, revert to "pensive Sara", the "belovéd woman". This reversion in itself might have been the making of the poem; for clearly one of its main themes is that the "pure

---

[1] The passages are taken by Richards (*op. cit.*, p. 148) closely together, as if they belonged to the same strain of thought. The fuller draft of 1797, in the Cottle–Rugby MS (*PW*, II, 1022–3, ll. 36–46), reads:

> And what if All of animated Life
> Be but as Instruments diversly fram'd
> That tremble into thought, while thro' them breathes
> One infinite and intellectual Breeze,
> And all in diff'rent Heights so aptly hung,
> That Murmurs indistinct and Bursts sublime,
> Shrill Discords and most soothing Melodies,
> Harmonious from Creation's vast concent—
> Thus *God* would be the universal Soul,
> Mechaniz'd matter as th' organic harps
> And each one's Tunes be that, which each calls I.
>
> But thy more serious Look a mild Reproof
> Darts. . . .

joy and calm delight"[1] of a happy sexual love are conditions of the receptive mood of tranquillity. But instead of reverting to this, and transmuting it in the light of the central experience the poem describes, Coleridge brings back Sara as an extremely narrow and governessy orthodox Christian:

> But thy more serious eye a mild reproof
> Darts, O belovéd Woman! nor such thoughts
> Dim and unhallow'd dost thou not reject,
> And biddest me walk humbly with my God.
> Meek Daughter in the family of Christ!
> Well hast thou said and holily disprais'd
> These shapings of the unregenerate mind.

He calmly accepts this rebuke, utterly repudiates the experience he has just had as "Bubbles . . . on vain Philosophy's aye-babbling spring" and, in the character of a redeemed sinner, thanks Christ who

> gave me to possess
> Peace, and this Cot, and thee, heart-honoured Maid!

This ending is difficult to accept even in the earlier version before *Sybilline Leaves*; because the vague Neo-Platonist speculation does not seem wholly incompatible with the scheme of Christian redemption. It is possible that the sudden *volte face* in that version is to be explained less by a wish to repudiate the doctrine than by an anticipation of the later thought about the possible origin of moral evil in "the streamy nature of association"—

> Full many a thought uncall'd and undetain'd,
> And many idle flitting phantasies,
> Traverse my indolent and passive brain.

It may be a moral suspicion of these uncurbed and unruddered associations which called out the demand for a "Faith that inly *feels*". But what is now evident is that the ending as it stands seems to involve a rejection also

---

[1] "To the Evening Star", l. 8; *PW*, I, 17. See Geoffrey Grigson, *The Harp of Aeolus*, pp. 31–5, where Richards's treatment of the poem is substantially followed.

of the vital personal experience which was added in 1817: it murders the new-born life.

The finest poem in this group is "Frost at Midnight";[1] and indeed it is one of the finest short poems in the language. I think it is much loved; it is certainly much praised; but even so I doubt whether it is adequately appreciated as the perfectly achieved work of art which it is. It has suffered even more than the other poems from piecemeal handling; it is so exceedingly quotable for extraneous reasons. Either for biographical purposes —to illustrate Coleridge's boyhood at Christ's Hospital, where he "saw nought lovely but the sky and stars"; or to illustrate his life in the little cottage on the street at Nether Stowey, where it was written; or to illustrate Hartley's life because of the prophecies about him contained in it: or else for expository purposes—to show the development of Coleridge's attitude to nature or his skill in describing its details, the poem has been lovingly dissected, and for many readers lost. It can, perhaps, be best approached by comparing it with the lines in Cowper's *Task* which have already been mentioned:

> Me oft has Fancy ludicrous and wild
> Sooth'd with a waking dream of houses, tow'rs,
> Trees, churches, and strange visages, express'd
> In the red cinders, while with poring eye.
> I gaz'd, myself creating what I saw.
> Nor less amus'd have I quiescent watch'd
> The sooty films, that play upon the bars
> Pendulous, and foreboding in the view
> Of superstition, prophesying still,
> Though still deceiv'd, some stranger's near approach.
> 'Tis thus the understanding takes repose
> In indolent vacuity of thought,
> And sleeps and is refresh'd. Meanwhile the face
> Conceals the mood lethargic with a mask
> Of deep deliberation, as the man
> Were task'd to his full strength, absorb'd and lost.
> Thus oft, reclin'd at ease, I lose an hour
> At ev'ning, till at length the freezing blast,

[1] *PW*, I, 240.

That sweeps the bolted shutter, summons home
The recollected pow'rs; and snapping short
The glassy threads, with which the Fancy weaves
Her brittle toils, restores me to myself.
How calm is my recess; and how the frost,
Raging abroad, and the rough wind endear
The silence and the warmth enjoy'd within! [1]

When Cowper moves from the ordinary firegazing to the particular matter of the "stranger", the details are so similar that it is impossible to think that Coleridge did not have these lines in mind. Both use the superstition that Coleridge described in his note by saying: "In all parts of the kingdom these films are called *strangers* and supposed to portend the arrival of some absent friend"; the "extreme silentness" of the Nether Stowey cottage is paralleled by "the silence and the warmth enjoy'd within"; both stress the severity of the frost outside, though for Coleridge there is no freezing "blast". But the value of the comparison lies in the contrast between the moods of mind and the two poetic methods. Cowper emphasises the utter indolence, the insignificance, of his mood and the quite false appearance of "deep deliberation" which he gives to others; and the verse in which he gives expression to this is, strictly, desultory and unshaped. The "indolent vacuity of thought" which is the core of Cowper's experience is curiously like the less vacuous, but still unorganised, indolence which Coleridge allowed Sara to reprove at the end of "The Eolian Harp". But in Coleridge's poem there is no question of deceit or of a lost hour; his thought acquires serious content as it moves, and the man is really tasked to his full strength. What makes "Frost at Midnight" an achieved artistic whole is the design, the organisation, in the movement of the thought.

The centre is the Ego, the "I"—the seeing, remembering, projecting mind—the man sitting in a cottage room at night. From the room the mind moves out, by stages, first to the physical context of weather and sound, then

[1] *The Task*, Bk. IV, "The Winter Evening", about a third of the way through.

to the village, then to the world—"all the numberless goings-on of life". Next with a swift contracting transition, unexplained, in the middle of a line (l. 13) it comes in again to the fire. The movement of the film on the grate suggests the very kind of movement which the mind itself is here making—"the idling Spirit By its own moods interprets".

But the film, the "fluttering *stranger*", sets the mind off again outside, now backwards in time, through memory. And in the schoolboy reminiscence the same process happens again that has already happened in the cottage. From Christ's Hospital the boy's mind goes both back and outwards to Ottery, then forwards and outwards to the possible visitor who might come to take him out from school. Just as the poem as a whole is anchored to the original cottage room with the "low-burnt" fire —a phrase which comes centrally in the first paragraph—so the Christ's Hospital paragraph is anchored in the central phrase which produces the image of the schoolboy:

> Awed by the stern preceptor's face, mine eye
> Fixed with mock study on my swimming book.

From the memory of school the mind next comes back to the cottage room, by comparison between the two childhoods. The reader casts back over the room and the whole original situation the richness which is now added by the explicit expression of affection for the child. The backward movement of the mind in time is then balanced by the forward movement in time to Hartley Coleridge's imagined future. They link on the contrast of what each saw or will see of nature—the London schoolboy seeing "nought lovely but the sky and stars", Hartley to see everything that nature has to give.

This leads into the short passage of six lines on the Theistic Metaphysic of Nature. More is not necessary; for this includes and justifies the whole poem. God is

> Himself in all, and all things in himself.

He is in all this too; the fire, the frost, the cradle, the

school, the sky, the stars, clouds, winds and mountains; he is in all the memory and all the movement.

The quiet transition to the last paragraph is one of the most beautifully effective things in the whole poem. It returns to the opening context of seasons, weather and sounds through the imagining of Hartley's future, and comes round fully at the end to "the secret ministry of frost", and the quietness of the winter night, with which it began.

Not only do the movements of the mind give the poem its design and unity; but the poem as a whole leaves us with a quite extraordinary sense of the mind's *very being*, in suspense, above time and space; the mind with all its powers of affection and memory, and its power of reading nature as the language of God.

The predominant emotion is the deep, tender affection for the child. That is important not only to this poem's origin and character, but also to Coleridge's theory of what poetry ideally is.[1]

The growth of the poem into this unity and seriousness can be watched in the variant readings which Coleridge successively tried and rejected at two of its most crucial points. The first group of important changes took place in and among the lines now numbered 19–25. In the rejected versions, the mind, contemplating the flapping film, is said to transfuse into lifeless things its own "will" or "volition" and its own "delights" or "pleasures"

> sometimes with deep faith
> And sometimes with fantastic playfulness,

and such mental activities are called

> curious toys
> Of the self-watching subtilizing mind.

These versions, which speak of "fantastic playfulness" or "wilful playfulness", plainly belong more closely to the insignificant and irresponsible mood of Cowper, and to the ending of "The Eolian Harp"; they tend to blame

---

[1] See Chapter vi, below.

and discountenance the way the mind is behaving. The first tightening of these lines did not happen till 1828, and it had the effect of letting the beginning explain the shape of the body of the poem. The present received text establishes a very delicate balance:

> Methinks, its motion in this hush of nature
> Gives it dim sympathies with me who live,
> Making it a companionable form,
> Whose puny flaps and freaks the idling Spirit
> By its own moods interprets, every where
> Echo or mirror seeking of itself,
> And makes a toy of Thought.

The spirit is now called "idling", but the thought of sympathy with the film is no longer called an "idle thought": and, though the word "toy" is kept, nothing is said to discredit toys. There is, properly, a "play" of mind; and the spirit, originally idling, is led by the dim sympathies with the film to extend and explore its own movement.

The second point of major change was the ending. In the version of 1798, lines 65–72 were virtually as now, and the poem then concluded:

Or whether the secret ministry of cold
Shall hang them up in silent icicles,
Quietly shining to the quiet moon,
Like those, my babe! which ere tomorrow's warmth
Have capp'd their sharp keen points with pendulous drops,
Will catch thine eye, and with their novelty
Suspend thy little soul; then make thee shout,
And stretch and flutter from thy mother's arms
As thou wouldst fly for very eagerness.

This was a stopping rather than an end; for once the vista of new domestic detail was opened there was no reason why it should not be indefinitely followed, with increasing shapelessness. This was informal and conversational as family talk. The decision to stop at line 74 was one of the best artistic decisions Coleridge ever made. For not only is the present ending one of the finest pieces of short descriptive writing in the language, intricate and yet at the same time sparsely clear, compressing so much of the moods of various weather; but it also perfectly rounds the movement of the mind which has been the poem's theme:

> Therefore all seasons shall be sweet to thee,
> Whether the summer clothe the general earth
> With greenness, or the redbreast sit and sing
> Betwixt the tufts of snow on the bare branch
> Of mossy apple-tree, while the nigh thatch
> Smokes in the sun-thaw; whether the eave-drops fall
> Heard only in the trances of the blast,
> Or if the secret ministry of frost
> Shall hang them up in silent icicles,
> Quietly shining to the quiet Moon.

CHAPTER IV

THE ANCIENT MARINER

I QUOTED in Chapter I, as an example of Coleridge's public prose style, the opening of the Prefatory Note to "The Wanderings of Cain"; it describes how that curious prose fragment came into being, and it ends by saying that the whole scheme for the collaboration with Wordsworth in a poem about Cain "broke up in a laugh: and the Ancient Mariner was written instead". This is only one among a number of partial records left by Coleridge himself, or by the Wordsworths, of the origin of the "Mariner". These different records piece together into a quite intelligible and consistent account, too familiar to repeat.[1] But "The Wanderings of Cain" has a special place in that account because it shows how the subject of terrible guilt, suffering, expiation and wandering was already in Coleridge's mind before the various hints which were to form the outline of the Mariner's story came together. Cain's "countenance told in a strange and terrible language of agonies that had been, and were, and were still to continue to be". These agonies were related to a landscape in tune with them:

The scene around was desolate; as far as the eye could reach it was desolate: the bare rocks faced each other, and left a long and wide interval of thin white sand.[2]

It is even verbally but a few steps to "the wide, wide sea".

In another draft fragment of the Cain poem[3] a rather obscure and evasive sentence says that God inflicted punishment on Cain "because he neglected to

[1] The other leading references are conveniently given in Lowes, pp. 222–4, 528–31. Cf. *BL*, Ch. xiv.
[2] *PW*, I, 289, ll. 67–72.   [3] *PW*, pp. 285–6, *n*. 1.

make a proper use of his senses, etc." Later in this draft come alligators and tigers in close conjunction, just as they occurred together in a speech of the Wandering Jew in Lewis's *The Monk*, which Coleridge reviewed in *The Critical Review* for February 1797.[1] The Mariner bears traces of both these two traditional figures, Cain and the Wandering Jew.[2]

Not only once, but twice, Coleridge and Wordsworth began to collaborate in an exceedingly light-hearted way in works which dealt with crime, guilt, expiation and wandering. If we are broadly able to trust Coleridge's account, "The Wanderings of Cain" was begun as a composition-race: and there is no reason at all to doubt that "The Ancient Mariner" was begun by them jointly to raise £5 to pay the expenses of a walking-tour. It was thus an entirely unexpected by-product of Coleridge's main poetical plans. Those plans were, as we saw from the letter to Cottle which I quoted in the last chapter, of Miltonic size and seriousness. There is evidence, as Professor R. C. Bald has shown,[3] for believing that he was deliberately reading with the idea of writing two main works, a series of Hymns to the Sun, Moon and Elements, and an Epic on the Origin of Evil. It is hardly necessary even to say how much matter in the "Mariner" overlaps with what might have gone into those two works.

We may even suggest that the accident, so to speak, of beginning the "Mariner" on that November evening in 1797 released Coleridge from some of the burden of his Miltonic responsibilities and helped to split his ambitious synthesising aim of bringing all human knowledge together in the frame of one or more huge poems. I have already tried to show how, in the more ambitious poems just before this period, he was attempting, without much success, to synthesise politics, religion and philosophy in a highly Miltonic style. Now the aims and material split. It has been observed by Dr. Tillyard how very unpolitical "The Ancient Mariner" is. "Frost

[1] This review is reprinted in *CMC*, pp. 370–8.
[2] For fuller details see Lowes, pp. 243–60.   [3] Bald, pp. 15 ff.

at Midnight" (dated February 1798—that is while the "Mariner" was still being written) is, if possible, less political still. It is interesting that Coleridge's best political poem, "France: an Ode", is also dated February 1798: creative energy used in one direction and style seems also to have released it in other directions and styles. A political Ode in the Gray/Mason tradition, and a blank-verse meditative poem, soaring right away from its origins in Cowper, were written in among work on the " Mariner", which differed from both. There could be no clearer disproof of the narrowness of Coleridge's poetic range than the fact that these three poems are contemporary.

Little need be said about the context of styles to which the "Mariner" belongs: it has plain affiliations with Gothic horrors, of which Lewis was the fashionable exponent; and it is noticeable too that in the original volume of the *Lyrical Ballads* "The Ancient Mariner" is the only poem which derives its style from the traditional ballads as they were then available in Percy, rather than from the later ballad of broadsheet.[1] The precision, success and care, with which Coleridge later cut out many of the cruder traces of these origins—the pseudo-antique spelling, the more glaring archaisms of vocabulary, some of the marvels—is fresh evidence of the justice of his detailed judgement: but yet, when all these changes had been made, it is still remarkable how many features of ballad idiom and method the poem still retains and completely assimilates, diverting and modifying them to its own particular effects. It is partly by these means that the poem manages to escape history and yet retain tradition. Though it will not tie to a table of dates or a map, the "Mariner" yet uses the keepings of European tradition and all the details of wind and weather which every map implies. Its imagery, both of religion and of the elements, goes deep

[1] See the Percy version of "The Wandering Jew"; "Sir Cauline" for some of the vocabulary; "Young Waters" and "King Estmere" especially for past tenses with "did". William Taylor's translation of Bürger's "Lenore" must not be forgotten.

below the surface of what we may happen to remember or happen to have seen.

But at the same time it uses to the full the vividness of visual description which was one of Coleridge's great poetic strengths. A friend of mine recently said he could not read Coleridge any more—no, not even "The Ancient Mariner": he could not stand all the supernatural part; but only a few sentences later he went on to say that on a slow sea-voyage to Africa he got up early and walked round the deck reciting the poem to himself, and that nothing could have better fitted his mood or described what he saw than

> The fair breeze blew, the white foam flew,
> The furrow followed free.[1]

Scarcely any reader, from first acquaintance in childhood, has not felt that the first, most elementary contact with the poem leaves such isolated descriptions fixed in the memory, and it is only a step further, if it is a step at all, to feel, at the next level of relevance, the perfect attunement between the descriptions and the states of the Mariner's mind.

> Down dropt the breeze, the sails dropt down,
> 'Twas sad as sad could be;
> And we did speak only to break
> The silence of the sea![2]

None of Coleridge's poems shows more completely developed in practice the principle of description which was quoted earlier from his letter to Sotheby of 1802:

Never to see or describe any interesting appearance in nature without connecting it, by dim analogies, with the moral world proves faintness of impression. Nature has her proper interest, and he will know what it is who believes and feels that everything has a life of its own, and that we are all *One Life*. A poet's heart and intellect should be *combined*, intimately combined and unified with the great appearances of nature and not merely held in solution and loose mixture with them, in the shape of formal similes.[3]

---

[1] ll. 103–4; all quotations from the "Mariner" are from the text in *PW*, I, 187–209.

[2] ll. 107–10. [3] *L*, I, 403–4; see above, pp. 54 and 75.

The full relevance of this to "The Ancient Mariner" will begin to appear gradually in what I have to say later. The present relevance is that in the poem the method of relating nature to the moral world is not by "dim analogies", nor "in the shape of formal similes" (there are very few), but by the poet's heart and intellect being intimately *combined* and unified with the great appearances of nature. The method of conjunction is immediate in the natural imagery, and it is only by understanding the imagery that the "moral world" can be understood. For the present a single simple instance must be enough.

> And now there came both mist and snow,
> And it grew wondrous cold:
> And ice, mast-high, came floating by,
> As green as emerald.
>
> And through the drifts the snowy clifts
> Did send a dismal sheen:
> Nor shapes of men nor beasts we ken—
> The ice was all between.
>
> The ice was here, the ice was there,
> The ice was all around:
> 't cracked and growled, and roared and howled,
> Like noises in a swound! [1]

In those stanzas it is *in* the descriptive phrases "As green as emerald" and "a dismal sheen" that the double mood of admiration and fear is conveyed: and the double character of this mood is important.

"The great appearances of nature" play an overwhelming part in the poem, and their part was emphasised and further explained in the prose gloss that was added in 1817. Lowes put this side of the poem epigrammatically by saying that the chief characters in "The Ancient Mariner" are "Earth, Air, Fire and Water".[2] By chief "characters" we must understand also chief channels of action—for it is through the elements that the Mariner is acted upon.

[1] ll. 51-62.   [2] Lowes, pp. 74 ff.

The function of the elements and heavenly bodies is not merely to *image* the Mariner's spiritual states (though indeed they do this), but also to provide in the narrative structure of the poem the link between the Mariner as ordinary man, and the Mariner as one acquainted with the invisible world, which has its own sets of values.

This link is first suggested in the idea that the Albatross has a power of control over the elements: it is continued in the idea of the plaguing spirit that followed the ship nine fathoms deep from the land of mist and snow. The skeleton ship with the figures of Death and Life-in-Death is linked to the phenomena of the tropical sunset:

> The Sun's rim dips; the stars rush out:
> At one stride comes the dark;
> With far-heard whisper, o'er the sea,
> Off shot the spectre bark.[1]

The angelic spirits who inspire the dead men to work the ship are sent to release the ship from the control of the daemons of the elements; and the spirit from the South Pole works under their orders. The two voices in Parts V and VI are two fellow daemons of the Polar Spirit, two "invisible inhabitants of the element", as the gloss calls them. And finally the ship is brought back to port under the undisputed control of angelic spirits, but accompanied by a wind.

Across this whole system of daemons of the elements and angelic spirits lies the framework of ordinary Catholic theology—Christ and Mary Queen of Heaven, and in the ending the ordinary Catholic practices of confession, absolution and church-going.

The inter-relation of the different spiritual beings is one of the hardest points in the poem to be clear or confident about; and it is best, approaching the more doubtful through the less, to begin by discussing the poem's more obvious bearings on the "moral world", and indeed to establish first that it has a bearing on the moral world at all. For even this has sometimes been disputed. We must start from Coleridge's one main

---

[1] ll. 199–202.

comment on the poem, as it is reported in the *Table Talk* under 31 May 1830:

Mrs. Barbauld once told me that she admired the Ancient Mariner very much, but that there were two faults in it,—it was improbable, and had no moral. As for the probability, I owned that that might admit some question; but as to the want of a moral, I told her that in my own judgment the poem had too much; and that the only, or chief fault, if I might say so, was the obtrusion of the moral sentiment so openly on the reader as a principle or cause of action in a work of such pure imagination. It ought to have had no more moral than the Arabian Nights' tale of the merchant's sitting down to eat dates by the side of a well, and throwing the shells aside, and lo! a genie starts up, and says he *must* kill the aforesaid merchant *because* one of the date shells had, it seems, put out the eye of the genie's son.

The story of the Merchant and the Genie in *The Arabian Nights* is briefly this. A merchant is travelling in a desert with nothing to eat but some biscuits and dates in a wallet. He sits down to eat dates and throws the stones about: a huge and terrible genie appears, with a great scimitar, and says he will cut off the merchant's head. Why? Because one of the stones was flung into the eye of the genie's son and killed him. The merchant pleads that it was quite accidental: but the genie is relentless. Finally the genie allows the merchant one year's respite. He is free to go home to provide for his wife and children, and to order his affairs. This he does, with great justice and generosity and, after a struggle, he returns to the same spot in the desert, as arranged with the genie, exactly one year later. Here he falls in with three old men, mysterious strangers, to whom he tells his story; the genie then appears again. And each of the strangers in turn makes a bargain with the genie that if he can tell the genie a story more marvellous than he has ever heard before, the genie is to remit one-third of the merchant's punishment. The stories cap each other for marvellousness; the genie is honest to the bargain; the merchant goes free and triumphant home, and the three old men go off mysteriously into the desert as they came.

Now this story has not got a "moral" in the sense that there is a clear explicit detachable maxim which neatly sums up the didactic drift of it. But it seems equally clear that one cannot possibly read the story without being very aware of moral issues in it; aware that its whole development is governed by moral situations, and that without them there wouldn't really be a story. The arbitrariness of the genie; the awful consequences to the merchant of what was originally, on his side, a pure accident; the thoughts of the merchant for his family; these are moral matters. The generosity and exactness with which he arranged his affairs in the year of respite is developed very fully in the story: and much is made of the struggle about his bargain to return, and of the punctuality and faithfulness with which he kept it. It is very difficult indeed, in reading the story, not to see in his final release, as the result of the three old men's tales, a reward for his honourableness and care in all his dealings. And when one has got so far, it is not difficult to see that—always allowing for the fact that no "maxim" conveys the *whole* moral of a story—some such maxim as this, deduced from it, is not irrelevant: "The arbitrary character of fate may be overcome by human honour and goodness; and there may be mysterious powers in the world which aid these virtues." In the *Arabian Nights* version this moral, or anything like it, is not in Coleridge's words "obtruded too openly". But to deny altogether that it (or something like it) is there (when the whole story depends on the genie's arbitrariness, the merchant's honourableness and his final release) would seem to me a grotesque example of wilful blindness.

We do not know how well Coleridge remembered the story or how accurately his nephew reported what he said. But as the *Table Talk* passage stands, it is surely clear that Coleridge never said or meant that the "Mariner" neither had nor was meant to have a moral bearing or a "moral sentiment". He said the fault was "*the obtrusion* of the moral sentiment *so openly* . . . in a work of such pure imagination". And this seems to point to his possible dissatisfaction with the summary of the "moral" as a kind of didactic epigram towards the end:

> He prayeth well, who loveth well
> Both man and bird and beast.
>
> He prayeth best, who loveth best
> All things both great and small;
> For the dear God who loveth us,
> He made and loveth all.[1]

It is obvious that those lines do rub the point home and that they may, when detached from their context, be degraded to the status of a motto in "almanac art", or used to express the quite worthy desire to put out crumbs for the dicky-birds on a cold and frosty morning. But coming in context, after the richness and terror of the poem, it is no more a banal moral apothegm, but a moral which has its meaning *because it has been lived*.

All recent full discussions of "The Ancient Mariner" have taken this for granted. In what follows I owe a great deal to three such discussions, one by Dr. Tillyard;[2] one by Dr. Bowra;[3] and one by the American writer and critic Mr. Robert Penn Warren.[4] All agree, however much they differ from each other, that the poem has a very serious moral and spiritual bearing on human life: and they are surely right. For Coleridge, talking in 1830, could not possibly have meant to exclude all moral relevance from the working of the "pure imagination" when his whole developed critical theory stressed again and again the union of heart and head, the special power of the poet to bring "the whole soul of man into activity."[5]

Coleridge has set us a special problem of critical method. It is obvious that his own creative experience must have deeply affected his critical theories and practice: but he never fully brought the two into relation; he rarely adduced his own poems as instances, and never expounded them. Furthermore, his important

[1] ll. 612-17.   [2] E. M. W. Tillyard, *Five Poems*, pp. 66-86.
[3] C. M. Bowra, *The Romantic Imagination*, Ch. iii.
[4] For full details, see List of Abbreviations, p. 12.
[5] *BL*, II, 12.

critical work was all a good deal later than most of his important creative work. We cannot thus be sure how much of his critical opinion may fairly be carried back into 1797–8 and brought to bear on his own greatest poetry. It is very hard to be fair, and not to pick out what suits us and reject the rest. It is, for instance, tempting to use Coleridge's later distinctions between allegory and symbol in interpreting "The Ancient Mariner"; but they had not been expressed in 1797–8. In fact, we may be misled if we start the critique of the "Mariner" and "Kubla Khan" with this disjunction of allegory from symbol in mind. For all allegory involves symbolism, and in proportion as symbolism becomes developed and coherent it tends towards allegory. This is one of the problems involved in Mr. Warren's exciting essay: he starts as a "symbolist" criticising all the "allegorisers" and ends up in something so organised and precise that Coleridge, anyway, would probably have called it an allegorisation. But Mr. Warren would be quite willing to accept that, provided only that his kind of allegory is seen to be distinct from simple "two-dimensional" allegory.

The poem's very richness at once tempts and defeats definiteness of interpretation; as we commit ourselves to the development of one strand of meaning we find that in the very act of doing so we are excluding something else of importance.

An example of this difficulty occurs on the threshold of interpretation, in the opinion we form about the Mariner's relation to ordinary human beings and the relation of the voyage to ordinary human life. Dr. Tillyard, struck (as everybody must be struck) by the similarities in spirit between the poem and the seventeenth-century voyages—

> We were the first that ever burst
> Into that silent sea—

as voyages of adventure and discovery, and using, to support his argument, the later Coleridge passage in the *Biographia* about the range of hills which must be crossed by an inquiring spirit, maintains that the Mariner himself is a mental and spiritual adventurer, "an unusually enquiring spirit", that he together with the rest of the crew are, from the accepted social point of view, *self-appointed* outcasts and criminals; and that the sea-voyage indicates "spiritual adventure" which they go out of their way to seek.[1]

But how is this present in the poem? The beginning of the Mariner's own account of the voyage contains no hint that he thought of the voyage as a high spiritual enterprise at variance with current limited social ideas, a conscious seeking of adventure. The ship starts off in an atmosphere of communal agreement and pleasure:

> The ship was cheered, the harbour cleared,
> Merrily did we drop
> Below the kirk, below the hill,
> Below the lighthouse top.[2]

The voyage, it seems, began normally, commonly, happily, the crew at one both with the society they left and with each other. In the literature of sea-going the antecedents are rather to be found in such voyages as that described by Herodotus—certainly used by Coleridge when he wrote

> The Sun now rose upon the right—[3]

the voyage in which the Phoenician seamen doubled the Cape without knowing that there was a Cape.[4] Adventure came upon them unaware.

The Mariner, said Wordsworth in rude complaint, "does not act, but is continually acted upon". There is, surely, an important element of truth in this, though it does not in the least derogate from the poem's merits.[5]

---

[1] *Five Poems*, pp. 70–1.   [2] ll. 21–4.   [3] l. 83.
[4] Hdt. IV, 42, 3–4. Coleridge would certainly have known the passage in the original, and also, as Lowes shows (p. 127), the quotation and application of it in Bryan Edwards's *History . . . of the British Colonies in the West Indies.*
[5] Wordsworth's famous, disingenuous and ungenerous note on the "Mariner" was published in *Lyrical Ballads* (1800), I, on an unnumbered page after the text; quoted in full, Lowes, p. 520.

There are only three points in the poem at which the Mariner may be said to "act"; these are—the shooting of the Albatross; the blessing of the water-snakes; and the biting of his arm. Each of these actions has a very different character. The shooting of the Albatross comes quite suddenly and unexplained; superficially it is unmotivated and wanton. The Mariner himself never makes any explicit attempt to explain it: nor does the poem contain, from his point of view, any defence of it. We shall return to this. In the first phase of his recovery, in the crisis at the centre of the poem, when he blesses the water-snakes, he does so *unaware*, and this word "unaware" is deliberately repeated and occurs each time significantly, emphatically, at the end of the line. That is to say, he did not really know what he was doing; he could find no adequate spring of action in himself, and retrospectively attributed his undeliberate blessing to a supernatural influence on him:

> Sure my kind saint took pity on me.[1]

He himself thought he was more acted upon than acting. Against this must be set the one clear occasion in the poem on which the Mariner does deliberately act. In Part III, when all the crew, including himself, have been stricken dumb by the drought, it is he who sees the sail; it is he who, by a prodigious effort, bites his arm, sucks the blood and finds voice to cry out. This is his one tremendous effort: it is a moment of terrible hope for him and for the whole crew. But the hope is blasted, not just negatively, but positively, appallingly, blasted. The crew all die cursing him with their eyes, and he alone survives.

This is crucial to the whole poem's dramatic effect and, by inference, also to its moral effect. On the one occasion when the Mariner does consciously, deliberately and with all his effort *act*, his action leads ironically to the climax of the disaster. The irony is enforced by the two lines that end this Part:

> And every soul, it passed me by,
> Like the whizz of my cross-bow![2]

[1] l. 286. [2] ll. 222–3.

The disastrous anticlimax of this action and this hope is made to throw back to the earlier, unexplained act of the shooting. (One main element in the poem's theme is that the Mariner's experience involves a tangle of error, incomprehensibility and frustration. He is certainly not a great courageous spiritual adventurer, though he has a great spiritual experience.) He started his voyage in unison with the ordinary world in a common set of values: he comes back as half outcast and half participator. In the poem as a whole a deliberate contrast is certainly presented between the background of the wedding and the Mariner's tale. The interruptions of the Wedding-Guest are meant to point this contrast. His constant fear is that the Mariner is a ghost come back from the dead or even himself some kind of infernal spirit. The contrast is not so much between two types of personality, the normal/conventional and the abnormal/adventurer, but between two aspects of reality, and two potentialities of experience, the visible bodily world of human beings marrying and giving in marriage and an invisible world of spirits and the dead where quite a different system of values is to be learnt. The effect of the interruptions of the Wedding-Guest is to show how these two kinds of reality are always co-existent: the total effect of the poem is to show them interpenetrating. As it has been said, in one aspect the poem is a prothalamium, and there is even the hint that though the wedding-guests who make the "loud uproar" have got their values wrong, yet the bride and bride-maids singing in the garden-bower are somehow touched by the Mariner's spiritual knowledge: and certainly the guest who has heard the tale cannot join the ordinary merry-making: "He went like one that hath been stunned".

The words "error" and "incomprehensibility", used just now of the Mariner's experience, were then a temporary and partial formulation of what must now be developed. The Mariner leaves his killing of the Albatross without any full explanation; he does not, cannot or dare not attempt to give his motives. But the description of the bird, its nature and power, taken with the

96

prose gloss, makes it clear that the killing of it was a ghastly violation of a great sanctity, at least as bad as a murder. The bird's human associations appear in the fact that it was hailed as a Christian soul in God's name, it answered the Mariner's hollo, ate human food, and played with the crew. The gloss calls it "the pious bird of good omen".[1] Thus it images not only its own obvious place in the natural order, but a system of both human and religious values which is declared to have power over the ship and its crew through its connection with the weather. Furthermore, a function of the bird as a Christian emblem is also hinted at later on, when its corpse is hung round the Mariner's neck "instead of the cross".

We have to consider our terminology for talking of an image used in such a complex way. Mr. Warren systematically and boldly uses the terms "symbol" and "symbolism", and develops his theory of a symbol as "focal, massive, and concrete"; Dr. Bowra also accepts the term "symbol". The terminology is not what matters so much as the degree of precision and equation that the use of a terminology allows. Mr. Warren is here somewhat confused: at one point he seems to equate the killing of the bird with the murder of a human being (arguing by a long analogy from Poe), and at another point to say that the killing "symbolises" the Fall. If these two things are to be held together, it is clear that the symbol must be functioning not merely towards different objects but in different ways: for the killing cannot *equate* with both a murder and the Fall, which are very different kinds of things. It seems best to avoid the term "symbol" in order to avoid this risk of incompatible equation. What happens in the poem is that the images gather their bearing by progressively rich associations, by gradual increment, and that exact equation is never fully demanded, even though the associations are ordered and controlled. The killing of the Albatross thus becomes a violation of a great sanctity at the animal, human, and spiritual levels: but these

[1] Coleridge's "Argument" to the edition of 1800 said the Mariner killed the bird "cruelly and in contempt of the laws of hospitality."

levels are only gradually declared as the poem proceeds, just as the Mariner only gradually discovered the consequences of what he had done. Our enlightenment runs parallel with his.

Any possible link with the Fall is of a different kind from the link with murder; for if such a link is there, it lies in the corruption of the human will by original sin and must be imported into the poem from outside, to explain the Mariner's motive, when he is not able or willing to explain it himself. His sin may or may not be partly the sin of pride and self-assertion against the order of the universe. As the poem stands it is a sin of ignorance, and links to that half-adumbrated sin of Cain, that he "neglected to make a proper use of his senses etc." It was a wicked ignorance because accompanied by a wildly thoughtless failure to consider what might be the truth about the order of the universe.

This failure to reach the truth, and, to him, the incomprehensibility of what was going on, is made more apparent when the rest of the crew become accomplices in his crime. They do not know whether the fog and mist (along with the Albatross who brought them) are good or bad, or whether the bird belongs more to them or to the breeze: nor do they know whether the sun is good or bad. This is made fully apparent in that wonderful pair of stanzas in which the thought and verse are in shape identical, but with opposite content:

> And I had done a hellish thing,
> And it would work 'em woe:
> For all averred, I had killed the bird
> That made the breeze to blow.
> Ah wretch! said they, the bird to slay,
> That made the breeze to blow!

> Nor dim nor red, like God's own head,
> The glorious Sun uprist:
> Then all averred, I had killed the bird
> That brought the fog and mist.
> 'Twas right, said they, such birds to slay,
> That bring the fog and mist.[1]

[1] ll. 91–102.

The best approach to clarifying these stanzas (and the poem as a whole) is through the nature of the sun.

In the very next stanza the misunderstanding and incomprehensibility are allied to the wonder at novelty which the poem took over from the sixteenth-century voyages:

> We were the first that ever burst
> Into that silent sea.

This is one of the places in which the parallel between the physical voyage and the spiritual experience is most perfectly realised. An experience you don't understand produces first a shock of new glorious delight and then turns out to be something else. It is the worst kind of ethical and spiritual mistake—accepting wrong values.

On the naturalistic level this turns on the character of the tropic sun: and much here depends on the syntax.

> Nor dim nor red, like God's own head,
> The glorious sun uprist:

The syntax of these two lines makes it possible to interpret—

Either (a) That God's head *is* dim and red, but the glorious sun uprose unlike it.
   Or (b) That the glorious sun rose like God's head which is *not* dim and red.

Interpretation (b) is made rather more likely, and (a) rather more unlikely, by the comma after "red", and this comma is apparently present in all texts. *Lyrical Ballads*, 1800, reads:

> Nor dim nor red, like an Angel's head,

with a comma after "head".[1] There seems no apparent

---

[1] *Lyrical Ballads* (1800), I, 162. The important comma after "Angel's head" is omitted in *PW*, I, 190, *apparatus criticus*. Warren at this point seems to be mistaken: he accepts interpretation (b) for the text, but then goes on to argue that the mariners have a wrong view of God because "dim and red" are qualities of the "other light" group, and belong with the luminous haze, etc. But surely "dim and

reason, either internally in the poem, or externally, why an angel's head should be dim and red. This temporary variant seems to point to accepting interpretation (b) with the common reading.

The very fact that Coleridge ever changed "God's own" to "an Angel's" seems to suggest that what he had in mind was the nimbus, aureole or "glory" of Christian iconography, and that this is picked up in the word "glorious". The rising sun was bright, golden and rayed, quite different from the small, clear-edged, bloody sun which becomes the image of evil two stanzas later. At the naturalistic level, both for the mariners and for Coleridge, the tropic sun changed from being a beautiful, pleasant, "good" thing to being an unpleasant, evil thing: this change is a natural quality of the tropic sun, irrespective of the eye of the beholder. The naturalistic error of the crew was not to know that the tropic sun has this double character: and this naturalistic error is an image of their moral and spiritual error. This brings clearly to the front a main feature of "the great appearances of nature" in the poem. It has been remarked for some time that the evil and disaster in the poem occur under the light of the sun, and the different phases of the redemption occur under the light of the moon. And Mr. Warren has developed this "symbolism of the two lights" further than it had been taken before, by the introduction of his "secondary" theme which I shall come to in a moment.

In Part II the becalming and the drought all occur under the influence of the sun; it is under the bloody sun that the deep rots, and that the creatures of the deep are slimy things that crawl with legs upon the slimy sea. We have already noticed how the spectre-bark appears in conjunction with the tropical sunset.

---

red" are an anticipation of the evil "bloody sun" that soon follows. Warren is far too exact in requiring every "dim" light to be "good"; and he underestimates the truth to physical fact about the tropic sun. See also Leo Kirschbaum, *The Explicator*, Vol. VII, No. 1, Oct 1948. I thank Mr. James Maxwell for this reference, which, in fact, introduced m⌐ to Warren's book.

Part IV begins with the crisis of extreme isolation, with the frustrated desire for death, and then moves into the first phase of recovery and redemption.

The parallels here again between the spiritual and the natural—the physical imagery not just illuminating but actually conveying the spiritual state—are what most characterise the poem. It is clearest in the landless waste of the sea, the most awful loneliness:

> Alone, alone, all, all alone,
> Alone on a wide wide sea!
> And never a saint took pity on
> My soul in agony.[1]

The transition also from the barren desire for death to the first state of redemption is brought in through the magnificent imagery of the moon and stars. From the helpless repetition of

> the sky and the sea, and the sea and the sky[2]

—the dead, static, unchanging monotony of the spiritual isolation without a specified light—there is a shift by means of the wonderful stanza

> The moving Moon went up the sky,
> And no where did abide:
> Softly she was going up,
> And a star or two beside—[3]

From death to life, or rather from death-in-life, which is so much worse than death that death is longed-for and unattainable. From death-in-life to life. From the flat, unchanging waste of the sea and the sky and the sky and the sea to the ordered, even movement, with grace and hope, of the moon and stars.

The prose gloss at this point is that one long sentence of astounding beauty:

In his loneliness and fixedness he yearneth towards the journeying Moon, and the stars that still sojourn, yet still move onward; and every where the blue sky belongs to them, and is their appointed rest, and their native country and their

[1] ll. 232–5. [2] l. 250. [3] ll. 263–6.

own natural homes, which they enter unannounced, as lords that are certainly expected and yet there is a silent joy at their arrival.

The emphasis there seems unmistakable; that the moon and the stars express order and joy. And the word "joy" was a key word for Coleridge to express the fullest and richest happiness in experience.[1]

By this moonlight we see the colouring of the water-snakes, and the blessing of them is by this moonlight:

> Beyond the shadow of the ship,
> I watched the water-snakes:
> They moved in tracks of shining white,
> And when they reared, the elfish light
> Fell off in hoary flakes.[2]

The beams of the moon have just before been said to fall "Like April hoar-frost spread". In Dorothy Wordsworth's Journal and again and again in Coleridge's descriptive prose this comparison between moonlight and hoar-frost or "hoariness" occurs. It was one of their common, agreed comparisons.

The blessing under moonlight is the critical turning-point of the poem. Just as the Albatross was not a mere bird, so these are not mere water-snakes—they stand for all "happy living things". The first phase of redemption, the recovery of love and the recovery of the power of prayer, depends on the Mariner's recognition of his kinship again with other natural creatures: it is an assertion and recognition of the other central principle in the letter to Sotheby:

that everything has a life of its own, and that we are all *One Life*.

And at that point the reminder of the sin against this principle is gone—

> The Albatross fell off, and sank
> Like lead into the sea.[3]

At this point we must pause and look back; for we have passed over a difficulty in the imagery of the sun and moon. If the moon is to be associated always with the good and the redemption, why is it that the crew die by the star-dogged moon at the end of Part III? It is difficult to explain this and yet support the idea of a consistently developing imagery in terms of the penance and redemption and reconciliation theme alone; and it is this point, together with others allied to it, that chiefly made me sympathetic to the idea behind Mr. Warren's secondary theme of the "Imagination".

The poem up to this point, that is Parts I to IV and the opening stanzas of Part V, taken together with the ending, Part VII, is relatively easy to interpret as a tale of crime, punishment and reconciliation, with the recovery of love in the blessing of the water-snakes as its climax. But the remainder of Part V and the whole of Part VI do not seem at first sight to have quite the same coherence and point. It is here that readers may still find "unmeaning marvels" and an elaborated super-natural machinery which dissipates concentration. There are wonderful details in the verse, some of the finest descriptions of all; but they may seem to fall apart and to have too little bearing on each other and on the whole. Many published accounts of the poem do not adequately face the implications of the detail in these Parts. It is therefore best to summarise shortly what happens.

The Mariner hears a roaring wind and sees the fires and lightning in the sky. But the ship moves on un-touched by the wind, and the reanimated dead men work it: a troop of blessed spirits has entered into them. These spirits make various music. The ship goes on, moved from beneath by the spirit of the South Pole. Through the Two Voices the Mariner learns that it is this Polar Spirit who requires vengeance for the Alba-tross's death, and that he will have more penance to do.

Part VI. The Voices say that the ocean is under the power of the moon. The ship is now moved northward by the angelic power while the Mariner is in his trance. He wakes to see the final curse in the eyes of the dead men. Then that spell is snapped, and he feels at last a sweet breeze on himself alone. He arrives at his home port, steeped in moonlight. Then, as the gloss says: "The angelic spirits leave the dead bodies, And appear in their own forms of light". This acts as the signal which brings out the boat from land.

In Part VII a dreadful rumbling sound comes under the water and the ship sinks.

A quite normally accepted and simple interpretation of Parts V and VI treats them as a further necessary extension of the expiation theme. In the blessing of the water-snakes the Mariner has reconciled himself to the creatures, but it remains for him to reconcile himself also with the Creator:[1] therefore he has to suffer once more (this time from the curse of the dead men's eyes) and to win the power of recognising the beauty of the angelic music.

This is broadly acceptable; but it takes us very little distance in understanding the complicated machinery. Is there any serious import in the answers to such questions as these: What is the function of the Polar Spirit? In one aspect he appears as the friend and avenger of the "pious bird of good omen", and yet he is made to work under obedience to the angelic troop, who are thus plainly, in the spiritual hierarchy, superior to him; and he is bought off by the promise that the Mariner's penance shall continue. It might have seemed better to have made the angelic troop themselves the protectors of the Albatross and made them require the further penance. Why should the ship be moved first by the Polar Spirit and then by the angelic power? Again, what is the significance of the two winds in Parts V and VI? Put the problem in another way: are the avenging by the tutelary spirits of the South Sea and the reanimation of the dead bodies to work the ship here just out of politeness, because Wordsworth suggested them?[2] The first main problem here is to decide whether there is any meaning in the two different kinds of supernatural being.

[1] See, e.g., Bowra, *op. cit.*, pp. 70-1.

[2] The Fenwick Note to "We are Seven", *Poetical Works*, ed. E. de Selincourt, I, 360-1; see also Lowes, pp. 222-3.

The whole discussion of this problem has been clarified and ennobled by Mr. Warren's long essay, which I now wish to summarise. He maintains that the poem has "two basic themes, both of them very rich and provocative". The primary theme, which is "the outcome of the fable taken at its face value as a story of crime and punishment and reconciliation", is the "the theme of sacramental vision, or the theme of the 'One Life'." The secondary theme is "concerned with the context of values in which the fable is presented" and is "the theme of the imagination". The two themes are finally fused in the poem.[1] He aims to establish the existence of this secondary theme by two lines of argument—first, that there are parts of the poem not otherwise easily intelligible, such as Parts V and VI; and second, that the symbolism of the poem is richer and more coherent than the redemption, visionary, theme alone requires. Mr. Warren elaborates the contrast of the "two lights" in great detail.

He points out quite rightly and fully (p. 87) the "pervasive presence of the moon and moonlight in Coleridge's work", especially in association with creativeness. In "Sonnet to the Autumnal Moon", 1788, she is called, the "Mother of wildly-working visions",[2] and in "Songs of the Pixies", 1796, "Mother of wildly-working dreams".[3] "Christabel" and "The Ancient Mariner" are bathed in moonlight: the moon is over the deep romantic chasm of "Kubla Khan"; it is prominent in "The Nightingale", "Cain" and "Dejection".

Mr. Warren maintains that the association is so recurrent and persistent in Coleridge's writing, between creation or the activity of the secondary imagination and the moonlight, half-lights, dim lights, gloom, luminiscent clouds and so on, that the association between them can

---

[1] Warren, p. 71. [2] l. 2; PW, I, 5.
[3] Warren here gives the publication date; the lines were written in 1793; PW, I, 40–4. The phrase quoted is in fact applied to Night, not to the Moon; ll. 85–7 are more relevant:

> What time the pale moon sheds a softer day
> Mellowing the woods beneath its pensive beam:
> For mid the quivering light 'tis ours to play.

justifiably be regarded as habitual; and that as it goes back even into his very early poems, it can without injustice be taken as established (even if not consciously) at the time of writing the "Mariner". He quotes from the *Biographia* passage in which Coleridge recalled the origin of the *Lyrical Ballads* themselves:

> The sudden charm, which accidents of light and shade, which moon-light or sun-set, diffused over a known and familiar landscape, . . . These are the poetry of nature.[1]

The Albatross, besides being associated with human nature on the level of the primary theme, is also associated with the moon, mist, cloud and fog-smoke, on the level of the secondary theme of the imagination:

> In mist or cloud, on mast or shroud,
> It perched for vespers nine;
> Whiles all the night, through fog-smoke white,
> Glimmered the white Moon-shine.[2]

Furthermore the bird is associated with the breeze, which Mr. Warren takes to be the "creative" wind, for which there are countless parallels in other poets.

> The sun is kept entirely out of the matter. The lighting is always indirect, for even in the day we have only "mist or cloud",—the luminous haze, the symbolic equivalent of moonlight. But not only is the moon associated with the bird, but the wind also. Upon the bird's advent a "good south wind sprung up behind". And so we have the creative wind, the friendly bird, the moonlight of imagination, all together in one symbolic cluster.[3]

He thus establishes what he calls a "symbolic cluster", including the wind, bird, mist and moon, which belong to the imagination and all the imaginative side of man's activity. And in his shooting, the Mariner not only commits a crime against the other, natural and spiritual, order of the world, but also a crime against creative imagination; and part of the penalty is the loss of the wind.

The dual character of the ice which I have already

[1] *BL*, II, 5.   [2] ll. 75–8.   [3] Warren, p. 91.

noted at the first arrival of the ship near the South Pole—
the emerald and the dismal sheen—also expresses the
dual character of the imagination, that it is partly a
blessing and partly a curse to him who lives by it.   It is
this cursing side of the imagination which accounts for
the particular vengeance of the Polar Spirit on the
Mariner as distinct from the punishment exacted by the
sun. And this dual character and special vengeance also
explain why the moon is allowed to be the light by which
the crew die.   And further, in his capacity of Wanderer,
the Mariner is to be thought of as the "cursed poet" of
the later Romantics. By contrast to the moon and
mist of the Imagination, the sun and the glaring light
are, for Mr. Warren, the light of the Understanding, the
mere reflective faculty, which "partakes of DEATH"; [1]
and just as the Mariner and also the crew failed to see
the significance of the bird in the mist, so they also fail
to understand the nature of the sun, not only at the
naturalistic level, as we have already seen, but also
because they are taking the lower faculty of the Understanding as their inadequate guide to life. [2]

Warren's essay must be read complete, with its notes,
to see how inadequate is this broad outline of its argument.
There are two main questions about it which most
urgently need asking: how far does it succeed in giving
a coherent and convincing explanation of the miscellaneous detail in the difficult parts of the poem? And in
what sense does it establish that there is a theme which
is "the theme of the imagination"? The answers to both
these questions depend upon the view we take of symbols
and symbolism.

I suggest that if we accept the term "symbol" we must

---

[1] Warren, p. 79 and *passim*, quoting *BL*, I, 98.

[2] Assuming that the sun does represent the Understanding, I
think Mr. Warren makes his own case more difficult than he need
when he comes to explain the appearance of the sun in a good context, when the angelic spirits fly up from the bodies into it. For
surely to Coleridge the Understanding was never altogether unnecessary in the whole scheme of the mind's action. It was never altogether superseded, but was always a necessary ground of advance
towards the Reason and the Imagination.

allow symbols a freer, wider, less exact reference; and that therefore it is probably wiser to drop the term altogether. Mr. Warren himself fully allows for the possibility (even likelihood) that Coleridge did not *consciously* use symbols at all. This is consistent with Coleridge's recognition of the unconscious element in the workings of genius: but it does not therefore follow that there was a latent precision waiting for critics to elucidate it. Mr. Warren seems in the last resort to be a precisionist more because he wishes to make clear to himself and others some features of the richness he has found in the poem than because he believes that the poem actually works upon its readers by the methods of precision. There is a natural and proper dread of the long-traditional praise of the poem's "atmosphere", because that praise has so often accompanied the belief that there is scarcely any content or meaning at all, and that all is thin, vague and "magical". But a rich certainty is not the only alternative to a poor uncertainty.

The first of the two questions, that about the miscellaneous detail, can only be answered here by two examples. In dealing with Part V, Warren agrees with Bowra and others that "in the reanimation of the bodies of the fellow mariners, there is implicit the idea of regeneration and resurrection"; but then he finds himself compelled to write:

But the behaviour of the reinspirited bodies, taken in itself, offers a difficulty. Taken at the natural level, the manipulating of the sails and ropes serves no purpose. Taken at the symbolic level, this activity is activity without content, a "lag" in the poem, a "meaningless marvel".[1]

Nor does he later succeed in giving an adequate explanation of the need for this behaviour, even when not "taken in itself"; for he concentrates more on the angelic troop than on what it makes the bodies do.

At this point Warren's scheme of symbolism does not serve us. But if we look to the total effect of the poem on its readers, there is little doubt that ll. 329–44 add

[1] Warren, p. 97.

something not adequately expressed elsewhere, especially the stanza:

> The body of my brother's son
> Stood by me, knee to knee:
> The body and I pulled at one rope,
> But he said nought to me.

This brings home, as nothing else does, the horror of the deaths, the violation of family ties which the action has involved; it dramatises to the Mariner's consciousness the utter ruin of the merry, unified community which had set out on the voyage. The curse in the stony eyes (ll. 436–41) is made far more appalling by this specially intimate experience of the fact that intimacy was gone for ever. And this is achieved at a point where the "system" of the poem is decidedly weak.

The second point of detail is the rumbling and the sinking of the ship in Part VII; Warren skates over this rather hastily:

There is the terrific sound which sinks the ship and flings the stunned Mariner into the Pilot's boat. In the logic of the symbolic structure this would be, I presume, a repetition of the wind or storm motif: the creative storm has a part in re-establishing the Mariner's relation to other men. Even if the destruction of the ship is regarded, as some readers regard it, as a final act of the Polar Spirit, to show, as it were, what he could do if he had a mind to, the symbolic import is not altered, for the Spirit belongs to the cluster of imagination which has the terrifying and cataclysmic as well as benign aspect.[1]

He then argues that the sinking of the ship is not an act of the Polar Spirit, but of the angelic troop.

At the level of the primary theme, the angelic troop wipe out the crime (i.e., the "criminal" ship and the dead bodies); at the level of the secondary theme, they do so by means of the "storm" which belongs to the symbolic cluster of the imagination.[2]

But this is surely to abandon a coherent symbolism altogether and to fall back on simple interpretation of

[1] Warren, p. 100. [2] *ibid.*

the narrative in the light of decisions already made; for the clusters of symbols established earlier have borne some intelligible relation (either traditionally or in Coleridge's habitual associations) to what they symbolise: the creative wind is traditionally intelligible, and the moon and half-lights have special associations for Coleridge. But the method of the ship's destruction does not conform to the "logic" of such symbolism as this; and Warren's use of "I presume" points to his uneasiness about it.[1] A submarine rumbling followed by a violent explosion is in a different key; it has a different sort of effect on the reader from that of the other items which Warren groups together as associated with the Imagination.

What seems to have happened is that Mr. Warren, delighted by the relative coherence of the moon-bird-mist-wind cluster, has forced other items into congruence with it, by minimising differences in their character and in their emotional effects. But such forcing would not have been necessary if he had started out with a less rigid theory of symbolic reference. That his own mind was working from the less precise towards the more precise, even in the course of thinking out his essay, is apparent in the way he speaks of the light of the sun. On p. 93 he writes of the sun:

It is the light which shows the familiar as familiar, it is the light of practical convenience, it is the light in which pride preens itself, it is, to adopt Coleridge's later terminology, the light of the "understanding", it is the light of that "mere reflective faculty" that "partook of Death".

His mind is here moving out of what is richly and variously suggestive into what is precise and technical. I suggest that he went through a similar mental process in reaching the interpretation of the moon, the bird and the mist, and that in the result the "theme of the imagination" is something narrower and more technical than the poem can carry. For by the imagination Warren does

[1] And his writing of the Mariner being flung into the boat by the sound suggests some hasty reading here.

mean the technical, creative poet's imagination of Coleridge's later theory, and he says (p. 103) that the poem is "in particular about poetry itself". This leads to the conception of the Mariner as the *poète maudit*.

The fact, however, is that there was for Coleridge no such stable and exact association between moonlight, half-light, shifting lights-and-shadows, etc. and the specifically poetic and creative imagination. These were indeed associated with and productive of creative and visionary moods, but they were also associated with the more tender emotions and the more fruitful virtues, such as those of love. These lines, addressed to Tranquillity in 1801

> And when the gust of Autumn crowds,
> And breaks the busy moonlight clouds,
> Thou best the thought canst raise, the heart attune,
> Light as the busy clouds, calm as the gliding moon.[1]

are part of the definition of a mood of moral insight which originally had a topically political context. This description of Hartley in a letter to Tom Poole in 1803 is expressive of the creativeness of a child's whole living personality, which may indeed bear analogies to poetic creativeness but yet, in a child, certainly cannot be identified with it:

> Hartley is . . . a strange strange Boy—"*exquisitely wild*"! An utter Visionary! like the Moon among thin Clouds, he moves in a circle of Light of his own making—he alone, in a Light of his own. Of all human Beings I never yet saw one so naked of *Self*.[2]

Again, the famous lines of "Dejection: an Ode"

> This light, this glory, this fair luminous mist,
> This beautiful and beauty-making power[3]

describe not the "shaping spirit of Imagination" itself, but the Joy which is the prerequisite condition of it. One more example brings us back closely to Mr. Warren's more limited application of the "symbolism" of the moon. In the lines "To William Wordsworth", written after hearing

[1] *PW*, I, 361   [2] *UL*, I, 292   [3] *PW*, I 365.

the first version of *The Prelude* read aloud, Coleridge describes himself while listening as being like the sea under the influence of the moon:

> In silence listening, like a devout child,
> My soul lay passive, by thy various strain
> Driven as in surges now beneath the stars,
> With momentary stars of my own birth,
> Fair constellated foam, still darting off
> Into the darkness; now a tranquil sea,
> Outspread and bright, yet swelling to the moon.[1]

Here there is no doubt that the moon is an image of Wordsworth's imagination seen in its power over others. By contrast, at the other extreme of reference, is the Note-Book entry

> Socinianism, moonlight; methodism, a stove. O for some sun to unite heat and light![2]

And in the intermediate, neutral area Coleridge once summed up his fascinated interest in the natural phenomena of a night-sky by applying to it the phrase of Boccaccio, *vestito d'una pallidezza affumicata*.[3]

It would be endless to quote all Coleridge's uses of imagery from the moon and stars, clouds, the night-sky and uncertain lights; these examples give some idea of the range. It is certain that, before and after the time of "The Ancient Mariner", such images were used for creativeness both of a wider and of a more specially poetic kind; but they were used also for much else, especially in conjunction with the subtler processes of the mind and the more delicate modes of feeling. They were used especially for the mysteries and uncertainties of mental life which Coleridge was beginning to explore more fully as he became more dissatisfied with the crude associationism represented by Hartley and its "inanimate

---

[1] ll. 95–101; *PW*, I, 408. Cf. Satyrane's First Letter in *The Friend*, 23 Nov 1809, quoted in *PW ad loc*. The patches of phosphorescent light in the sea-foam are an image of Coleridge's troubled, but bright, reception of those moments in *The Prelude* in which he himself was involved.

[2] *AP*, p. 26   [3] *ibid.*, p. 46.

cold world", and as his general ideals of life moved further from those of "the poor loveless ever-anxious crowd". It seems to me that the imagery of the mist and the moon and the Albatross in "The Ancient Mariner" belongs with this area of experience in general and with Coleridge's exploration of it; indeed the whole poem is part of the exploration, it is part of the experience which led Coleridge into his later theoretic statements (as of the theory of the Imagination) rather than a symbolic adumbration of the theoretic statements themselves.

Within the poem, and most obviously in the motto later added from Burnet ("Harum rerum notitiam semper ambivit ingenium humanum, nunquam attigit."), the emphasis is on the mystery and the richness of the mystery. Through the development of the imagery we are gradually led into the realisation that the values of "the land of mist and snow" are of the greatest possible concern, but that they are indescribable. They are certainly contrasted with the values which belong to the specious day-to-day clarity of the sun, but they are left to establish themselves in us mysteriously and indefinitely, as Burnet's world of spirits is mysterious and indefinite. Mr. Warren has permanently enriched our understanding of the poem by insisting on its statement of the "context of values" in which the crime and punishment and re-conciliation occur; his symbolist "equations" serve to point out elements which may be involved in this context; but the decision to "adopt Coleridge's later terminology" in stating the equivalents symbolised has, in the long run, the effect of making the poem seem more technical and diagrammatic than Mr. Warren himself first found it, or than Coleridge could ever have admitted it to be.

CHAPTER V

KUBLA KHAN, CHRISTABEL AND DEJECTION

IF Coleridge had never published his Preface, who would have thought of "Kubla Khan" as a fragment? Who would have guessed at a dream? Who, without the confession, would have supposed that "in consequence of a slight indisposition, an anodyne had been prescribed"? Who would have thought it nothing but a "psychological curiosity"? Who, later, would have dared to talk of its "patchwork brilliance"?[1] Coleridge played, out of modesty, straight into the hands of critics.

Were it not for Livingston Lowes, it would hardly still be necessary to point out the poem's essential unity and the relation between its two parts. But Lowes's book has such deserved prestige for other reasons that his view may still have undeserved currency. He treats the relation between the parts as "inconsequential".

With utter inconsequence, as the caves of ice glance and are gone, the Abyssinian damsel with a dulcimer is there, a tantalising phantom of a dream-remembered dream, unlocalized, without the slightest sense of unreality, in space; while the Tartar youth with flashing eyes is projected against the background of that twice phantasmal dome in air, dreambuilt within the dream. It is a bafflingly complex involution —dreams within dreams, like a nest of Oriental ivories, "sphere in sphere".[2]

He also talks of the "vivid incoherence" of the second part.[3] This shows, more clearly than anything could, the prejudice under which readers labour from having

---

[1] P. H. B. Lyon, *The Discovery of Poetry*, p. 101.

[2] Lowes, p. 409.

[3] *ibid.*, p. 363, where it is called an attribute of dreams.

been told beforehand that the poem was a dream, or the result of a dream. For it is exactly on the relationship between these two parts that the poem's character and the whole interpretation of it depend.

The "flashing eyes and floating hair" could only have been attributed to a "Tartar youth" by somebody who had momentarily forgotten the *Phaedrus*, say, and *A Midsummer Night's Dream*. For this is poetic frenzy, and the "symphony and song" are the emblemised conditions of poetic creation. The unity of the poem focuses on just that transition from the first part to the second, and the pivot of all interpretation is in the lines:

> Could I revive within me
> Her symphony and song,
> To such a deep delight 'twould win me,
> That with music loud and long,
> I would build that dome in air. . . .[1]

For "Kubla Khan" is a poem about the act of poetic creation, about the "ecstasy in imaginative fulfilment".[2] Interpretations have diverged to opposite poles of major meaning on the treatment of the emphasis and rhythm of that single line—"Could I revive within me". If a strong emphasis (and therefore necessarily also a strong metrical stress) is put upon "could", the word can be taken to imply "If only I could, but I can't", and the whole poem can be made to appear to be about the failure and frustration of the creative power. But if the emphasis on "could" is slight, then the condition is an "open" condition, like "Could you make it Wednesday instead of Thursday, it would be easier for me"; and the matter is the very possibility of creative achievement. The word "once" in the line "In a vision once I saw" then also becomes a light syllable, not implying "Once, only once and, I fear, never again", but rather indicating delight, surprise and the sense of unique privilege.

In this choice I have no hesitation in taking the second alternative; not only is it biographically relevant to point out that in 1797-8 Coleridge, so far from be-

[1] *PW*, I, 298.   [2] Maud Bodkin, *Archetypal Patterns in Poetry*, p. 95.

moaning the loss of creative power, was only just dis-
covering its strength; but also the whole rhythmic
character of the paragraph requires this view. The
metre is light and fast; the paragraph moves from
delight and surprise, through enthusiasm to ecstasy;
no sensitive reader can read it otherwise. The verse is
asserting, not denying, the ecstasy. If this were a poem of
frustration and failure, the movement would be slow and
the stresses heavy. Another verbal detail points the same
way—"I would build *that* dome in air". What dome?
Of course, the dome that has been described in the first
part. And if it had not there been fully described, the
music of the singing and the dulcimer would not have
any substantial and evident power. It is just because the
first part presents the dome and the river with all its
setting so completely, beautifully and finally, that we
accept the authenticity of the creative impulse in the
second part, and find in the last word "Paradise" a fact,
not a forlorn hope. "Kubla Khan" is a triumphant
positive statement of the potentialities of poetry. How
great those potentialities are is revealed partly in the
description of its *effects* at the ending of the second part
and partly in the very substance and content of the first.

The precision and clarity of the opening part are the
first things to mark—even in the order of the landscape.
In the centre is the pleasure-dome with its gardens on
the river bank: to one side is the river's source in the
chasm, to the other are the "caverns measureless to
man" and the "sunless sea" into which the river falls:
Kubla in the centre can hear the "*mingled* measure" of
the fountain of the source from one side, and of the dark
caves from the other. The river winds across the whole
landscape. Nobody need keep this mere geographical
consistency of the description prominently in mind as he
reads (though once established it remains clear and
constant); but I suggest that if this factual-visual consistency had been absent, and there had been a mere
random sequence or collocation of items, such as a
dream might well have provided—items which needed a
symbol-system to establish relations at all—then the

absence *would* be observed: the poem would have been quite different, and a new kind of effort would have been needed to apprehend what unity it might have had. Within this main landscape, too, there is a pervasive order. The fertility of the plain is only made possible by the mysterious energy of the source. The dome has come into being by Kubla's decree: the dome is stately; the gardens are girdled round with walls and towers.

It is so often said that "Kubla Khan" achieves its effect mainly by "far-reaching suggestiveness", or by incantation or by much connotation, with little denotation, that it is worth emphasising this element of plain clear statement at the outset, statement which does particularise a series of details inter-related to each other, and deriving their relevance from their inter-relation and their order. Furthermore, the use of highly emotive and suggestive proper names is proportionately no large source of the poem's effect; it is only necessary to watch the incidence of them. Xanadu, Kubla Khan and Alph occur once in that form within the poem's opening two-and-a-half lines: and none of them occurs again except for the single repetition of Kubla in line 29. Abyssinian and Mount Abora occur once each, in the three lines 39–41. There are no other proper names in the poem at all, unless we should count the final word Paradise.

Next, the mode of appraisal which relies on suggestiveness is likely to underestimate the strength and firmness of the descriptions. In particular, lines 17–24, describing the source of the river, do not in method employ "suggestiveness" at all.

> And from this chasm, with ceaseless turmoil seething,
> As if this earth in fast thick pants were breathing,
> A mighty fountain momently was forced:
> Amid whose swift half-intermitted burst
> Huge fragments vaulted like rebounding hail,
> Or chaffy grain beneath the thresher's flail:
> And 'mid these dancing rocks at once and ever
> It flung up momently the sacred river.

We may well believe that this is based on a combination

of William Bartram's description of the "chrystal fountain" with his description of the "Alligator Hole",[1] but he did not provide the organisation of the words to convey so fully the sense of inexhaustible energy, now falling now rising, but persisting through its own pulse. We have here in verse the counterpart to such later prose descriptions as that of the starlings or the "white rose of eddy-foam". The whole passage is full of life because the verse has both the needed energy and the needed control. The combination of energy and control in the rhythm and sound is so great, as in

> at once and ever
> It flung up momently the sacred river

that we are even in danger of missing the force of the imagery, as in "rebounding hail" and "dancing rocks". If we miss it, it is our fault not Coleridge's; and it sometimes appears as if readers are blaming or underestimating him because they have improperly allowed themselves, under the influence of the rhythm, to be blind to the "huge fragments" and "dancing rocks" which lay another kind of weight upon it, and to be blind to the construction of the thought, which holds together the continuity and the intermission.

A different kind of clarity and precision in the first part leads us nearer to the poem's central meaning—the consistency with which the main facts of this landscape are treated, the dome and the river. The dome (apart from the biographists' concern about its oriental connection with opium—all the more important to them because Purchas did not mention it and archaeologists have found no trace) is an agreed emblem of fulfilment and satisfaction, it is breast-like, full to touch and eye, rounded and complete. In the first part it is mentioned three times, as "a stately pleasure-dome" in line 2, as "the dome of pleasure" in line 31, and as "A sunny pleasure-dome" in line 36. Each time the word "pleasure" occurs with it. So too, the word *river* is used three times in the first part, and each time, without fail,

---

[1] Lowes, pp. 367–9; *PW*, I, 297.

it is "the *sacred* river": this is its constant, invariable epithet. The centre of the landscape of this part is, as we have seen, the point at which the dome and the river join:

> The shadow of the dome of pleasure
> Floated midway on the waves.

Here, without possibility of doubt, the poem presents the conjunction of pleasure and sacredness: that is the core of Part One. And in Part Two the poet who has been able to realise this fusion of pleasure and sacredness is himself regarded as a holy or sacred person, a seer acquainted with the undivided life: and this part is clinched by the emphatic and final word Paradise. The conditional form of Part Two does not annul the presentation of Paradise in Part One, though it may hold out the hope of a future fuller vision.

What is this Paradise? Those who are intent on making "Kubla Khan" either a poem about imaginative failure or a document for the study of opium dreams, remind us that many of the sources for Coleridge's details were descriptions of false paradises; there was Aloadine's trick Mohammedan Paradise to which young men were lured and entertained with music and girls, so that they might be willing to die in battle in the hope of winning such joys for ever. There were, still more notably, the pseudo-Paradises of Milton,

> that faire field
> Of *Enna*,[1]

and the place

> where *Abassin* Kings thir issue Guard,
> Mount *Amara*, though this by som suppos'd
> True Paradise under the *Ethiop* Line
> By *Nilus* head.[2]

Of course we have in "Kubla Khan" a fruit of Coleridge's Miltonising, which I discussed in an earlier chapter, but because the Abassin kings and Mount

---

[1] *Paradise Lost*, IV, 268–9.   [2] *ibid.*, 280–3.

Amara belong with one false paradise it does not follow that the Abyssinian maid and Mount Abora belong with another.

There is only one answer to those who want to make this a false Paradise—that is, an appeal to the poem as a whole, its rhythmical development, its total effect as a poem of fulfilment, and to say "If you still want to make that experience a spurious experience, do so: 'Thy way thou canst not miss, me mine requires'." Acceptance of the Paradise, in sympathy, is the normal response, from childhood and unsophistication to criticism: to most people rejection would mean a ruinous and purposeless wrench. But what is being accepted?

Positively, it causes a distortion of the poem if we try to approximate this Paradise either to the earthly Paradise of Eden before the Fall or to the Heavenly Paradise which is the ultimate abode of the blest. It may take its imagery from Eden, but it is not Eden because Kubla Khan is not Adam. Kubla Khan himself is literally an oriental prince with his name adapted from Purchas. We may, if we persist in hankering after formal equations, incline to say he *is* the Representative Man, or Mankind in general: but what matters is not his supposed fixed and antecedent symbolic character, so much as his activity. Within the landscape treated as literal he must be of princely scope, in order to decree the dome and gardens: and it is this decree that matters, for it images the power of man over his environment and the fact that man makes his Paradise for himself. Just as the whole poem is about poetic creation at the imaginative level, so, within the work of the imagination, occurs the creativeness of man at the ethical and practical levels. This is what the poet, of all men, is capable of realising.

I have already noticed that the name Kubla is repeated only once after the first line; and the place of its repetition is significant:

> And 'mid this tumult Kubla heard from far
> Ancestral voices prophesying war!

This is essential to the full unity of the conception: the

Paradise contains knowledge of the threat of its own possible destruction. It is not held as a permanent gift; the ideal life is always open to forces of evil; it must be not only created by man for himself, but also defended by him. It is not of the essence of this Paradise that it must be lost; but there is a risk that it may be lost.

About the river, again, we need not aim to be too precise and make equations. Its function in the poem is clear. The bounding energy of its source makes the fertility of the plain possible: it is the sacred given condition of human life. By using it rightly, by building on its bank, by diverting its water into his sinuous rills, Kubla achieves his perfect state of balanced living. It is an image of these non-human, holy, given conditions. It is not an allegorical river which would still flow across that plain if Kubla was not there. It is an imaginative statement of the abundant life in the universe, which begins and ends in a mystery touched with dread, but it is a statement of this life as the ground of ideal human activity.

The "caves of ice" need special attention. Some discussions of the poem seem to imply that they belong with the "caverns measureless to man"; but there surely can be no doubt that in the poem they belong closely and necessarily with the dome.

> It was a miracle of rare device,
> A sunny pleasure-dome, with caves of ice!

The very line shows the closeness by the antithesis, the convex against the concave, the warm against the cold. It is not necessary to invoke Coleridge's own statement of the theory of the reconciliation of opposites in art [1] ("the heat in ice" is even one of his examples) to see that it is the holding together of these two different elements in which the miracle consists. They are repeated together, also within the single line, 47, in Part Two. Lowes shows clearly how in Coleridge's memory the caves of ice came to be associated with the

---

[1] "On Poesy or Art", printed in *BL*, II, 255–6; *cf. BL*, II, 12.

sacred river [1]; and in his sources the ice does not indicate terror or torment or death (as Miss Bodkin [2] seems to think Coleridge's ice does here), but rather the marvellous, and the delight which accompanies the marvellous; the ice is linked specifically to the fountains sacred to the moon. This marvellousness is present also in "Kubla Khan", but there is more: ice is shining, clear, crystalline, hard: and here it adds greater strength and austerity to what would be otherwise the lush, soft, even sentimental, core of the poem. As it is, the miracle of rare device consists in the combination of these softer and harder elements. And when this is seen in relation to the act of poetic creation, in the light of which all Part One must be understood, its function is still plainer: such creation has this element of austerity in it.

For this is a vision of the ideal human life *as the poetic imagination can create it*. Part One only exists in the light of Part Two. There may be other Paradises, other false Paradises too: but this is the creation of the poet in his frenzy. And it is because he can create it that he deserves the ritual dread.

II

The critique of "Christabel" is an entirely different matter: for not only is it inescapably a fragment, but the two parts differ so much from each other, that they scarcely seem to belong to the same poem. The unlikeness here would have been altogether apparent even if Coleridge had not himself, as usual, used a Preface to explain that the two parts were written in different years, with the visit to Germany between them, and even if all his letters and other comments on the business were unknown.

One of the most obvious differences between the two parts is caused by his physical move from Somerset to the Lake District. In Part I there is the castle in the woodland, with oak and moss and mistletoe, a landscape which has its function only in relation to the persons and the atmosphere. There are no proper names but those

[1] Lowes, pp. 379–80.   [2] *Archetypal Patterns in Poetry*, p. 135.

of the three main persons. In Part II we plunge straight into the detailed geography of the region; Wyndermere, Langdale Pike, Dungeon-ghyll, Borodale and the rest, organise the reader's attention as if this were matter of history rather than of imagery.

It is generally agreed that the experience of reading the First Part of "Christabel" is more an acquaintance with an atmosphere than the apprehension of a poetic unity. This atmosphere is achieved partly through description of the setting, partly by the mystery surrounding Geraldine.

One of the familiar examples of description will illustrate also a point mentioned in passing in Chapter II, the relationship between Coleridge's descriptions and Dorothy Wordsworth's.

Dorothy, 25 January 1798:

> The sky spread over with one continuous cloud, whitened by the light of the moon . . .[1]

Dorothy, 31 January:

> When we left home the moon immensely large, the sky scattered over with clouds. These soon closed in, contracting the dimensions of the moon without concealing her.[2]

Coleridge, Gutch Memorandum Book:

> Behind the thin
> Grey cloud that covered but not hid the sky
> The round full moon looked small.[3]

Coleridge, "Christabel", Part I, lines 14–19:

> Is the night chilly and dark?
> The night is chilly, but not dark.
> The thin gray cloud is spread on high,
> It covers but not hides the sky.
> The moon is behind, and at the full;
> And yet she looks both small and dull.

We do not know whose original observation this may have been, but one thing is clear—that Coleridge did

[1] *Journals of Dorothy Wordsworth*, ed. E. de Selincourt, I, 4.
[2] *ibid.*, I, 5.   [3] Quoted in *C*, p. 3.

more than merely take over an existing observation of Dorothy's or his own, and transfer it straight into "Christabel"; because he has very much modified his own first verse draft in the Gutch book. Especially by adding the moon's dullness—perhaps he even did pronounce the word "dull" to rhyme with "full"—he has increased the mysteriousness and vagueness of the midnight light, and has reached an effect which is altogether absent from Wordsworth's lines in "A Night-Piece", which also belong with the same entry in Dorothy's Journal. Wordsworth wrote:

> The sky is overcast
> With a continuous cloud of texture close,
> Heavy and wan, all whitened by the Moon,
> Which through that veil is indistinctly seen,
> A dull, contracted circle, yielding light
> So feebly spread that not a shadow falls,
> Chequering the ground.[1]

The difference of atmosphere from "Christabel" is very marked. The whole Wordsworth poem is an attempt to expand, rather in the manner of Cowper, according to a method in which rhythm has little part; to win assent to the delight by mere accumulation of circumstance and detail. But in the result there is no particularity of mood. The Coleridge lines, by contrast, suggest both by vocabulary and rhythm that cloud and moon are behaving oddly and ominously, just out of the way of ordinary behaviour, as if proportion is thrown out and normal vision perplexed. At point after point in "Christabel" descriptions are used to heighten the mystery by such suggestions of slight distortion in behaviour, or of contrast, or surprise—

> And wildly glittered here and there
> The gems entangled in her hair.

in moonshine cold

> The brands were flat, the brands were dying,
> Amid their own white ashes lying;

[1] *Poetical Works*, ed. E. de Selincourt, II, 208.

But when the lady passed, there came
A tongue of light, a fit of flame;
And Christabel saw the lady's eye

The silver lamp burns dead and dim.

But it is all fragmentary and finally unsatisfying because it leads up to a mystery which is both incomplete and clueless. The enigmatic Geraldine entirely swamps Part I. I do not propose to go into the questions of how far she was a vampire or a Lamia or whether she was a victim of metempsychosis.[1] But Ernest Hartley Coleridge was surely right when he said that there are a number of indications that in Part I Geraldine is "at the mercy of some malign influence not herself".[2] She is in "sore distress" and asks for pity (l. 73); "in wretched plight" (l. 188); she first (apparently without irony) wishes Christabel's mother were there, and even after the malignant wish for the mother to be off, she will still try to requite Christabel well; she must even pray: "for I Must pray, ere yet in bed I lie" (ll. 233–4). The critical act of revealing her bosom is approached with extreme reluctance. She acts "drawing in her breath aloud Like one that shuddered". Then comes the main passage on which Ernest Hartley Coleridge comments:

> Ah! what a stricken look was hers!
> Deep from within she seems half-way
> To lift some weight with sick assay,
> And eyes the maid and seeks delay;
> Then suddenly, as one defied,
> Collects herself in scorn and pride,
> And lay down by the Maiden's side![3]

These lines did not occur in the original version of 1816;

[1] For an exhausting exploration of these questions, see Nethercot, Bk. II.

[2] *C*, p. 76 *n*. 2. But Gillman (p. 284) calls her "an evil being, not of this world".

[3] ll. 256–62; the earlier versions read, simply, for these lines:

> She took two paces and a stride,
> And lay down by the maiden's side.

they were not published till 1828; and that edition is the basis of the *textus receptus*. They occur in none of the main manuscripts. Their insertion seems rather to underline what was already implied, than to declare a later change of purpose; and they were, further, a protection against the misrepresentation of critics.

The whole of this scene has unquestionably a genuine horror in it: the mitigating explanatory lines were absent from the version reviewed so malignantly in *The Examiner* (very probably by Hazlitt) on 2 June 1816:

There is something disgusting at the bottom of his subject, which is but ill glossed over by a veil of Della Cruscan sentiment and fine writing—like moon-beams playing on a charnel-house, or flowers strewed on a dead body.

An anonymous pamphlet later "pronounced poor Christabel 'the most obscene Poem in the English Language'"—which prompted Coleridge's comment: "I saw an old book at Coleorton in which the Paradise Lost was described as an 'obscene Poem', so I am in good company." [1]

There are three extant accounts of how "Christabel" was to have been finished that are near enough to Coleridge himself to have serious claim to be considered authentic. Two come from Gillman, in whose house at Highgate Coleridge lived from 1816 till his death; the other from Coleridge's son Derwent. The shorter Gillman account is this:

The story of Christabel is partly founded on the notion, that the virtuous of this world save the wicked. The pious and good Christabel suffers and prays for

"The weal of her lover that is far away,"

exposed to various temptations in a foreign land; and she thus defeats the power of evil represented in the person of Geraldine. This is one main object of the tale. [2]

The Derwent Coleridge account is also short and general:

[1] *UL*, II, 247; *To* Southey, February 1819. The letter also says: "It seems that Hazlitt from pure malignity had spread about the Report that Geraldine was a Man in disguise."

[2] Gillman, p. 283.

The sufferings of Christabel were to have been represented as vicarious, endured for her "lover far away"; and Geraldine, no witch or goblin, or malignant being of any kind, but a spirit, executing her appointed task with the best good will, as she herself says:—

> All they, who live in the upper sky,
> Do love you, holy Christabel, &c. (ll. 227–32).

In form this is, of course, accommodated to "a fond superstition", in keeping with the general tenour of the piece; but that the holy and the innocent do often suffer for the faults of those they love, and are thus made the instruments to bring them back to the ways of peace, is a matter of fact, and in Coleridge's hands might have been worked up into a tale of deep and delicate pathos.[1]

The longer Gillman account of the projected third and fourth parts is this:

Over the mountains, the Bard, as directed by Sir Leoline, "hastes" with his disciple; but in consequence of one of those inundations supposed to be common to this country, the spot only where the castle once stood is discovered,—the edifice itself being washed away. He determines to return. Geraldine being acquainted with all that is passing, like the Weird Sisters in Macbeth, vanishes. Re-appearing, however, she waits the return of the Bard, exciting in the mean time, by her wily arts, all the anger she could rouse in the Baron's breast, as well as that jealousy of which he is described to have been susceptible. The old Bard and the youth at length arrive, and therefore she can no longer personate the character of Geraldine, the daughter of Lord Roland de Vaux, but changes her appearance to that of the accepted though absent lover of Christabel. Next ensues a courtship most distressing to Christabel, who feels—she knows not why—great disgust for her once favoured knight. This coldness is very painful to the Baron, who has no more conception than herself of the supernatural transformation. She at last yields to her father's entreaties, and consents to approach the altar with this hated suitor. The real lover returning, enters at this moment, and produces the ring which she had once given him in sign of her

---

[1] C, p. 52, n. 1: from *The Poems of Samuel Taylor Coleridge*, ed. Derwent and Sara Coleridge, [?] 1870. This undated issue first contained an introductory essay by Derwent Coleridge. I have not seen a copy of it, and C is my only authority for the quotation.

betrothment. Thus defeated, the supernatural being Geraldine disappears. As predicted, the castle bell tolls, the mother's voice is heard, and to the exceeding great joy of the parties, the rightful marriage takes place, after which follows a reconciliation and explanation between the father and daughter.[1]

James Dykes Campbell said in his edition of the poems (1893) that he suspected and hoped Coleridge was merely quizzing Gillman with the shorter account of the ending.[2] Dante Gabriel Rossetti took the longer Gillman ending seriously.[3] In two modern American articles it has been accepted as highly probable.[4] But the chief objection against the long Gillman ending is plain —that, as it is presented, it makes the story seem like a vulgar, trivial Gothic Romance; and Donald R. Tuttle has virtually accepted the idea that it is simply as a Gothic Romance that the poem is to be read. The shorter Gillman account of the ending, and the account given by Derwent Coleridge, both agree in making Christabel the centre of the main interest; and agree moreover on the view that the primary subject of the poem was Christabel's vicarious suffering for her lover.

This leads to the one other interesting recorded remark made by Coleridge himself about the poem— that Crashaw's verses on St. Theresa beginning

> Since 'tis not to be had at home,
> She'l travel to a martyrdome

were ever present to my mind whilst writing the second part of Christabel; if, indeed by some subtle process of the mind they did not suggest the first thought of the whole poem.[5]

Now since the central theme of the Crashaw poem is the desire for martyrdom, and since the traditional

[1] Gillman, pp. 301–2.   [2] p. 604.

[3] Hall Caine. *Recollections of Dante Gabriel Rossetti* (1882), p. 154.

[4] *Studies in Philology*, XXXIII, July 1936, B. R. McElderry Jr., "Coleridge's Plan for Completing *Christabel*".

P.M.L.A. LIII, June 1938, Donald R. Tuttle, "*Christabel* Sources in Percy's *Reliques* and the Gothic Romance".

[5] *Letters, Conversations and Recollections of S. T. Coleridge*, edited by Thomas Allsop, 3rd edn. (1864), pp. 104–5.

view of martyrdom, and of the virtue in the blood of martyrs, includes the idea of the value to others of vicarious suffering, this one remark of Coleridge's tends strongly to reinforce the evidence of Derwent Coleridge and the shorter account given by Gillman.

A. H. Nethercot, whose book *The Road to Tryermaine* contains the fullest and fairest modern attempt to interpret the poem, found himself forced in his conclusion to the belief that its theme was relatively "simple and straightforward". He argues that "Christabel" was to exemplify the "preternatural", just as "The Ancient Mariner" was to exemplify the "supernatural". Coleridge used the word "preternatural" at the beginning of his critique of *The Monk*: in 1801 he was planning to publish "Christabel" with two essays prefixed, one on the Preternatural and one on Metre.[1] Nethercot links this to the lines on Joan of Arc in "The Destiny of Nations", which speak of "Beings of higher class than Man", who take on human form for their own purposes, and make

> Of transient Evil ever-during Good
> Themselves probationary, and denied
> Confess'd to view by preternatural deed
> To o'erwhelm the will, save on some fated day.[2]

Geraldine, Nethercot argues, is such a being as this, in Derwent Coleridge's words, "a spirit, executing her appointed task with the best good will". She is the agency through whom Christabel (whose name has "Christ's name in 't") is to be brought to "an abbreviated but concentrated form"[3] of martyrdom at her father's castle. By this means Christabel would make atonement for the wrongs committed by her absent lover.

This is neat, and consistent with various evidence; but, as Nethercot fully admits, it is hard to reconcile with

---

[1] *L*, I, 349; To Thomas Poole, 16 Mar 1801. See Nethercot, pp. 200–1.

[2] *PW*, I, 136 *n*. The text is that included in Southey's *Joan of Arc*, 1796. See Nethercot, pp. 201–5.

[3] Nethercot, p. 210.

Coleridge's overwhelming difficulties in completing the poem, his references to his "vision" of it, all the suggestions that the theme was subtle and complicated. The underlying fact is that none of Coleridge's poems at this period can be covered by a short, neat statement of their theme, any more than "The Ancient Mariner" is explained by quoting the epigrammatic moral at its end. In view of Coleridge's statement about the importance to him, in a "subtle" way, of Crashaw's poem on St. Theresa, there seems a strong likelihood that he was hampered by problems which belong to the psychological borderland where matters of religion overlap with matters of sex:

> Shee never undertooke to know,
> What death with love should have to doe
> Nor has shee ere yet understood
> Why to show love shee should shed blood.

In the seventeenth century such double references could be carried together in the mind without any intellectual unease, and without any moral shame or awkwardness. In 1800 that was not so. Yet Coleridge, of all Englishmen then living, was the one most likely to have had some understanding of this borderland, and to have known intimately the difficulties of using that, perhaps dim, understanding at the centre of a narrative poem. He was not writing an elementary story of Gothic horror, but was trying to explore more deeply the serious psychological areas which such stories just touched in their own trivial way.

III

I do not mean to discuss the metre of "Christabel" or the controversies which have arisen from Coleridge's note upon it. But it is worth pausing to call attention, in an interlude, to the part which metrical experiment played in Coleridge's life. Many of his experiments were published by his grandson, and the Note-Books contain a number of discussions of metrical forms and theories which have not yet been printed.

Along with many others from Harvey and Spenser to Clough and Robert Bridges, he was interested in the experimental adaptation of classical Greek and Latin metres to English verse. He did this partly as Clough did, for a joke:

Read with a nod of the head in a humouring recitativo

made a good hexameter. But these lines about his hexameters themselves carry the effectiveness a good deal further:

All my hexameters fly, like stags pursued by the stag-hounds,
Breathless and panting, and ready to drop, yet flying still onwards,
I would full fain pull in my hard-mouthed runaway hunter.[1]

And altogether beyond this they sometimes reveal poetic achievement of a special kind. This comes about, I think, because the mere exercise of trying to produce English verses in classical metres gave him a sort of mental distraction from the *duty* of poeticising his thoughts, which was so often his greatest handicap; he was too intellectually clever. But to write hexameters or hendecasyllables acted on him like the use of a rosary on the ideal Catholic, providing a focus for distractions so that the heart-felt stream of prayer might flow. For Coleridge the attention to the metrical ingenuity acted just like that; it kept his mind off the conscious poeticising of his thoughts and left them free to run, in much the same way as for different reasons in "Kubla Khan" they ran. There is one passage which seems to me most of all to bear this out: and to be very relevant to other matters we have already discussed. It is from the hexameters in the letter to William and Dorothy Wordsworth which I have already been quoting, written from Ratzeburg in the winter of 1798–9 to them at Goslar. He had been suffering from a pain in his eyes; he had written to his wife: "a stye, or something of that kind, has come upon and enormously swelled my eyelids, so that it is painful or improper for me to read or write".

[1] *PW*, I, 304–5.

Then in the hexameter verses to the Wordsworths he wrote:

Five long hours have I tossed, rheumatic heats, dry and flushing,
Gnawing behind in my head, and wandering and throbbing about me,
Busy and tiresome, my friends, as the beat of the boding night-spider.

So much alone is impressive as a description of the state of pain. But after saying in the letter "I forget the beginning of the line", he continues, with a wonderfully expressive diagnosis of the relation of blindness to sight:

         . . . my eyes are a burthen,
Now unwillingly closed, now open and aching with darkness.
O! what a life is the eye! what a strange and inscrutable essence!
Him that is utterly blind, nor glimpses the fire that warms him;
Him that never beheld the swelling breast of his mother;
Him that smiled in his gladness as a babe that smiles in its slumber;
Even for him it exists, it moves and stirs in its prison;
Lives with a separate life, and "Is it a Spirit?" he murmurs:
"Sure it has thoughts of its own, and to see is only a language."

"And to see is only a language." What a brilliant insight this is into experience! It is not philosophy, but it is the expression of the concrete experience which is the ground of philosophy. It links to that Note-Book entry about looking over the Barnard Castle bridge:

What would it be if I had the eyes of a fly!—What if the blunt eye of a Brobdignag!—[1]

What if I had no working eyes at all? To see is only a language. This comes as the finish of a sequence of thought, where it could hardly be bettered. The relativity of visual experience is a familiar theme, one which Coleridge often explored; but here he slips out in unpremeditated verse a far deeper critique of the

[1] See above, pp. 56 and 75–6.

senses; and it was unpremeditated just because he was playing a metrical game; and it had its immediate origin in illness.

IV

For nearly sixteen years now the original full text of "Dejection: an Ode" has been known.[1] But the current editions and selections of Coleridge's poems still necessarily print the *textus receptus*, and consequently the relation between the various versions is not widely known and its import not generally understood. The *textus receptus* is called an Ode; it is divided into eight stanzas, which altogether amount to 139 lines. But the original version was written as a verse letter to Sara Hutchinson on 4 April 1802, in 340 lines: it is here reprinted in an Appendix for convenience.

The whole matter of these original "verses" and of the resulting Ode belongs so closely with that long prose entry in a Note-Book which I quoted in the first chapter that I would like just to refer to what I then said: the passage is a long meditation on personal unhappiness, with this at its centre:

O Sara wherefore am I not happy! Why for years have I not enjoyed one pure & sincere pleasure! one full joy!—one genuine Delight, that rings sharp to the Beat of the Finger!— all cracked, & dull with base Alloy!—

I said that there, in the rough, is the kind of personal experience from which there grew his insistence on the distinction between the primary and the secondary imagination: and that the secondary imagination appears not in its achievement—for the "recreation" is here "rendered impossible"—but in its "essentially vital" activity, as it "*struggles* to idealise and unify". In such prose passages we are watching a half-act of artistic creation.[2]

In the various stages of "Dejection: an Ode" we can, I

[1] Ernest de Selincourt, "Coleridge's *Dejection: an Ode*", *Essays & Studies*, XXII, 1937; and also de Selincourt, *Wordsworthian and other Studies*, pp. 57–76. See below, App. I, p. 157.

[2] See above, pp. 24–6.

think, see these "struggles" working on very similar material, carried into further stages towards artistic creation, towards unity. I think it is the opinion of many readers of the Ode, that brilliantly successful as most of it is, as *parts*, yet it fails to achieve complete artistic unity. By comparison with "Frost at Midnight" or "The Ancient Mariner" or "Kubla Khan" it is not a whole poem.

In the received text, the opening of Stanza VII especially, and its placing and relevance, are serious obstacles to accepting the poem as a whole. The stanza opens with a sudden twist of thought, in very awkward language:

> Hence, viper thoughts, that coil around my mind,
>   Reality's dark dream!
> I turn from you, and listen to the wind,
>   Which long has raved unnoticed.[1]

And the "viper thoughts" against which this revulsion occurs are the famous meditative stanza about the loss of his "shaping spirit of Imagination", ending with the lines:

> Till that which suits a part infects the whole,
> And now is almost grown the habit of my soul.

The phrase "reality's dark dream" then applies to the firm, sad honesty of self-analysis which make the greatness of that stanza. This result has come about by taking over the word "dream" from the original version (l. 185), where the "dark distressful Dream", from which he turns, is the thought of his misery if Sara were ill in body or in mind and he, necessarily absent, were unable to comfort her. The "dream" was not the honest self-analysis at all. And in the original version the passage about the loss of "the shaping spirit of imagination", though substantially the same in wording, follows, instead of preceding, the vital change in the weather: it follows the groans, and smarting wounds and the screams of the lost child. The "tender lay" is not

---

[1] ll. 94–7; *PW*, I, 367.

Otway's, but William's. The course of the weather is very important to the argument, and they move parallel.

Another major change is this: in the published Ode the praise and description of "joy" is divided between Stanza v and the end of Stanza viii, at the end of the poem. In the original verses these two parts are undivided, and form one long strain, at the end of the poem, a strain of forty-four lines, beginning

> O Sara! we receive but what we give,

including the images of the wedding garment, the shroud, the luminous cloud, the light, the glory, the fair luminous mist; and these images focus not on Coleridge and his loss of joy, but on Sara and her possession of it. It is thus a paean to her happiness, not a wail over his misery. Moreover, this long strain contains one important and beautifully developed image which was dropped altogether in the published version:

> Thou being innocent and full of love,
> And nested with the Darlings of thy Love,
> And feeling in thy Soul, Heart, Lips, and Arms
> Even what the conjugal and mother Dove,
> That borrows genial Warmth from those, she warms,
> Feels in the thrill'd wings, blessedly outspread—[1]

The loss of this from inside the praise of joy is perhaps the worst the poem has suffered. "Thy Soul, Heart, Lips, and Arms" and "the thrill'd wings" make the union of the physical and emotional in the mood of joy more concrete than anything retained in the public poem. In its original place the "conjugal and mother Dove" stood as a contrast to a long explicit passage about Coleridge's unhappiness in his own marriage,

---

[1] App. I, ll. 325–30; *cf.* for both theme and imagery these lines from "To Two Sisters" (1807), ll. 1–5; *PW*, I, 410:

> To know, to esteem, to love,—and then to part—
> Makes up life's tale to many a feeling heart;
> Alas for some abiding-place of love,
> O'er which my spirit, like the mother dove,
> Might brood with warming wings!

those habitual Ills
That wear out Life, when two unequal Minds
Meet in one House and two discordant Wills; [1]

about the fact

> that my coarse domestic Life has known
> No Habits of heart-nursing Sympathy.

In the light of these passages the line "Ours is her Wedding Garment, our's her Shroud" acquires its force: the two garments may be the same.

The main theme of the unpublished passages of the verses was the contrast between Sara Hutchinson's "joyous" membership of the Wordsworth group, with its permanency of gladness and affection, and Coleridge's own separation from it, and lack of an equivalent—

> To *visit* those, I love, as I love thee,
> Mary, and William, and dear Dorothy,
> It is but a temptation to repine—
> The transientness is Poison in the Wine,
> Eats out the pith of Joy, makes all Joy hollow,
> All Pleasure a dim Dream of Pain to follow! [2]

All this personal detail had to be cut out before publication, and in the cutting the sequence of the poem was altered as well as its direction and tone.

As the poem originally stood, the relation of the change in weather to the sequence of mood was quite different. The crescent moon and the " Green Light that lingers in the West" were the setting of the "stifling, drowsy, unimpassion'd Grief" ; of "I see, not feel, how beautiful they are"; of

> I may not hope from outward Forms to win
> The Passion and the Life, whose Fountains are within!

just as they are in the received text; the first, more quiet, mood of self-analysis. This passes on to the pain that he has caused Sara, to the happiness of the Wordsworth group, and to the dream of his absence from Sara in illness, which I have mentioned. The change in the

[1] App. I, ll. 243–5.   [2] *ibid.*, ll. 157–62.

wind has been happening "unnoticed" during these thoughts. The fierce, active variable wind then breaks in, and governs all the rest of the poem. The wind that is the "Mad Lutanist", the "Actor, perfect in all tragic Sounds", the "mighty Poet, even to frenzy bold", is the wind which leads into the lines about the suspense of imagination, the "abstruse research", and into the final forty-four lines about the power of joy inside the soul itself, the "strong music in the Soul",

> This Light, this Glory, this fair luminous Mist,
> This beautiful and beauty-making Power!

This wind has several different aspects: as tragic actor, and bold mighty poet it may express the wounds and groans of a host in rout together with a "Tale of less Affright, And tempered with Delight": but it is also the destructive wind from which regeneration may follow, at once destroyer and creator. The line

> And be this Tempest but a Mountain Birth

which now, slightly altered, comes in Stanza VIII, originally preceded the "Imagination" lines: the imagination has not come into the matter before that point.[1]

A case cannot be made out for the full coherence of the original version; but this major difference is important. For it is under the stimulus of this strong creative wind that the deepest self-analysis occurs, and also the fullest realisation of the power of joy, as it is actually achieved in Sara herself.

In the longer version, too, the Eolian harp is less prominent; the lines given to it are in length and substance virtually the same as in the shorter poem; and its function is rather to declare the character of the wind than to poise the doubtful question of the passivity or activity of the mind. I. A. Richards's long discussion of the harp image in *Coleridge on Imagination* [2] was written before the longer text was available; but he has since

---

[1] See Appendix II, p. 166.　　　　　[2] Esp. pp. 150, ff.

expressed (more or less) his adherence to what he then said.[1]

There will be something more to say about the harp image in the final chapter. But now I would suggest that the emphasis on it and on Coleridge's modes of imagining the relation between the mind and external nature, the treatment of his poems too much as embryo philosophy, has tended to obscure the place of the affections and feelings in them. "Dejection: an Ode" is not primarily a poem about modes of perception. It is a poem about unhappiness and about love and about joy. Of the later autobiographical poems there is least of self-pity in it, the self-analysis being all the clearer and more mature therefore, because the sense of love and of joy is so strong. This idea of joy was a guiding principle of Coleridge's life.

The "joy" of "Dejection" must be understood as involving the "deep delight" which "Kubla Khan" shows at the centre of creative happiness. To give some further indication of what "joy" meant to Coleridge I shall quote two entries in one of his Note-Books: the first comes before the writing of "Dejection" and describes a particular kind of joy in his son Hartley with splendid distinction:

Sunday, November 1. 1801. Hartley breeched—dancing to the jingling of the money—but eager & solemn Joy, not his usual whirl-about gladness—but solemn to & fro eager looks, as befitted the importance of the æra.[2]

That belongs partly with the "Conclusion to Part II" of "Christabel", and partly looks forward to "Dejection" in the following year. The other note was written after "Dejection", probably in October 1803, and applies to himself:

I write melancholy, always melancholy: you will suspect that it is the fault of my natural Temper. Alas! no.—This is

---

[1] *The Portable Coleridge*, ed. I. A. Richards (Viking Press, New York, 1950), pp. 15–16, 41–2.
[2] MS Note-Book No. 21. Add. MSS 47518, ff. 34v–35.

the great Cross in that my Nature is made for Joy—impelling me to Joyance—& I never—never can yield to it.—I am a genuine *Tantalus*—[1]

That is one of the most aweful things he ever wrote.

I said in Chapter I that there are passages in the later autobiographical poems where one can put one's finger on a word, phrase or rhythm which declares, in its poetic weakness, an emotional weakness which suddenly obtrudes, as if it came there through a lack of alert attention. And I suggested also that this weakness is often due to self-pity. It is the Tantalus who cannot reach his Joy.

Self-pity is exceedingly hard to sympathise with, to understand, to assess; it is easy to sweep it all away as undignified whining, lacking control and decorum, as evidence of a deep and distasteful psychological malaise. There are many parts of Coleridge's published writings, especially in his letters, which it is tempting to treat in this way. And he does suffer by comparison with others. There are many parallels, for instance, between his circumstances and those of Hopkins: both suffered from ill-health, the sense of isolation, and from a thwarting of the creative impulse; both planned or began many works which were never finished; both were faced, though in rather different ways, with the problem of bringing their creative poetical powers into relation with their scholarship and their technical interest in philosophy. Coleridge might well have taken as the motto or the basis of a poem that passage from the twelfth chapter of Jeremiah which opens Hopkins's sonnet:

> Thou art indeed just, Lord, if I contend
> With thee; but, sir, so what I plead is just.
> Why do sinners' ways prosper? and why must
> Disappointment all I endeavour end? [2]

In fact, this very idea is expressed in the ending of Coleridge's "Pains of Sleep", of 1803—

---

[1] MS Note-Book No. 21. Add. MSS 47518, ff. 70v–71.
[2] *Poems*, 3rd edn., ed. W. H. Gardner, p. 113.

> Such punishments, I said, were due
> To natures deepliest stained with sin,—
> For aye entempesting anew
> The unfathomable hell within,
> The horror of their deeds to view,
> To know and loathe, yet wish and do!
> Such griefs with such men well agree,
> But wherefore, wherefore fall on me? [1]

And his sonnet "Work without Hope" exactly parallels
Hopkins's contrast of the fertility and life of nature with
his own eunuch-like unproductiveness; "birds build, but
not I build", wrote Hopkins: and Coleridge—

> All Nature seems at work. Slugs leave their lair—
> The bees are stirring—birds are on the wing—
> And Winter slumbering in the open air,
> Wears on his smiling face a dream of Spring!
> And I the while, the sole unbusy thing,
> Nor honey make, nor pair, nor build, nor sing. [2]

The parallels in the circumstances, the ideas, even the
images are striking. But the comparison is in Hopkins's
favour, because he avoids just that kind of weakness. In
that stanza from "The Pains of Sleep", it is only in the last
line that they appear. Where Hopkins twice boldly uses
the strong interrogative "Why"

> Why do sinners' ways prosper? and why must

Coleridge twice side-by-side uses the weak interrogative
"wherefore"; it occurred in the verses to Sara, it occurred
in the prose meditation of October 1803; and here it
comes twice at the critical point in a stanza otherwise
strong and terrible:

> wherefore, wherefore fall on me?

It is a tone which his admirers have to face.

But the ending of the verses to Sara as a paean of joy
was not an isolated break from a lasting mood of self-pity.
She was for several years his focus-point and stay, and I

[1] ll. 43–50; *PW*, I, 390–1.
[2] Dated in first draft 21 Feb 1825; *PW*, I, 447 and II, 1110–1;
Hopkins may well have known this sonnet, and also "The Pains of
Sleep".

should like to end this chapter by quoting without comment the sonnet he wrote to her in 1801:

> Are there two things, of all which men possess,
> That are so like each other and so near,
> As mutual Love seems like to Happiness?
> Dear Asra, woman beyond utterance dear!
> This Love which ever welling at my heart,
> Now in its living fount doth heave and fall,
> Now overflowing pours thro' every part
> Of all my frame, and fills and changes all,
> Like vernal waters springing up through snow,
> This Love that seeming great beyond the power
> Of growth, yet seemeth ever more to grow,
> Could I transmute the whole to one rich Dower
> Of Happy Life, and give it all to Thee,
> Thy lot, methinks, were Heaven, thy age, Eternity![1]

[1] *PW*, I, 361-2. First published 1893. This sonnet was prefixed to the MS of "Christabel" which Coleridge presented to Sara Hutchinson.

CHAPTER VI

CREATION, EMOTION AND WILL

To say that this last chapter is to be about Coleridge's Criticism is too ambitious; for it will discuss only a few main points in his critical theory and practice which link to what has already been said about his personality and poems, and try to bring together some thoughts and suggestions left isolated or incomplete in the earlier chapters, in the hope that it may also, however slightly, help towards seeing Coleridge as a whole. His own experience and his own self-analysis gave the direction and character to his critical thought far more than anything he learnt from Kant and Schelling; and it is this experience, and his description and analysis of it, that I shall use as illuminating some of the formulated critical doctrine.

In discussing Coleridge's personality I said that his extreme illness and his unhappiness in personal relations intensified his habit of introspection, and brought him to write that *"all* the subtler parts of one's nature must be *solitary.* Man exists herein to himself and to God alone—yea! in how much only to God! how much lies *below* his own consciousness." [1] So he came to discover in himself the part of the unconscious in art and life. Its place in art he expressed most memorably in saying: "There is in genius itself an unconscious activity; nay, that is *the* genius in the man of genius". [2] His view of this, and its connection with the "streamy nature of association" is what I now want to explore.

It has long been plain from the *Biographia* and *Anima Poetæ* that his own introspective knowledge of this "streamy" nature of association underlay his rejection of

---

[1] See above, p. 44, quoting *AP*, p. 31.
[2] *CMC*, p. 210: Lecture xiii of 1818.

"associationism" as a theory of knowledge and as the basis of aesthetics. He knew too much about it, and suspected that the streamy nature of association might even be the origin of moral evil: at least he knew it could be the source of immoral actions in himself. Thus a note of impatience often comes into his critiques of associationism. On the mention of Alison's *Essays on the Nature and Principles of Taste* he writes:

Association in philosophy is like the term stimulus in medicine; explaining every thing, it explains nothing; and above all, leaves itself unexplained. It is an excellent charm to enable a man to talk *about* and *about* any thing he likes, and to make himself and his hearers as wise as before.[1]

He is writing also with introspective knowledge there. The following defines his position more clearly:

Seeing a mackerel, it may happen, that I immediately think of gooseberries, because I at the same time ate mackerel with gooseberries as the sauce. The first syllable of the latter word, being that which had co-existed with the image of the bird so called, I may then think of a goose. In the next moment the image of a swan may arise before me, though I had never seen the two birds together. . . . The accident of seeing two objects at the same moment acts as a distinguishable cause from that of having seen them at the same place: and the true practical general law of association is this; that whatever makes certain parts of a total impression more vivid or distinct than the rest, will determine the mind to recall these in preference to others equally linked together by the common condition of contemporaneity.[2]

The whole critique of associationism, as a theory, whether that of Hartley or of others, is built on the rejection of the mind's passivity, and of the Eolian harp as an image of the mind. The classical passage of rejection is also in the seventh chapter of the *Biographia*:

The Grimalkins in the Cat-harpsichord . . . did form a part of the process; but, in Hartley's scheme, the soul is present only to be pinched or *stroked*. . . . Accordingly, this "caput mortuum"

---

[1] *On the Principles of Genial Criticism* (1814), reprinted *BL*, II, 222.
[2] *BL*, I, 86–7; Ch. vii.

of the Hartleian process has been rejected by his followers, and the consciousness considered as a *result*, as a *tune*, the common product of the breeze and the harp: though this again is the mere remotion of one absurdity to make way for another, equally preposterous.[1]

An even more emphatic rejection occurs in a marginal comment on Kant:

The mind does not resemble an Aeolian harp, not even a barrel-organ turned by a stream of water, conceive as many tunes mechanized in it as you like, but rather as far as objects are concerned a violin or other instrument of few strings yet vast compass, played on by a musician of Genius.[2]

This occurs in a highly technical context—the critique of Kant's "manifold of sense".

The theory was rejected, partly because the fact of association was, for Coleridge, of such pre-eminent importance. On this Livingston Lowes engineered *The Road to Xanadu*. It must be remembered that Lowes built a great deal on his firm conviction that whereas "The Ancient Mariner" exhibits "superb, unwavering imaginative control" and is a coherent, unified poem, "Kubla Khan" is inconsequential, incoherent and not unified. I hope my fifth chapter made clear that this is not so, and that it is exactly the coherence, unity and strength of "Kubla Khan" that are striking: and that they would never have been doubted but for Coleridge's unnecessary confession about the dream. Lowes's misreading of "Kubla Khan" governed his whole approach to "the streamy nature of association which thinking curbs and rudders"; his treatment of the matter tended to approximate the "streaminess" always to the dream process, and to equate the "imagination" with the "thinking" which curbs and rudders. The imagination thus tended to become the ally of full normal consciousness and selective acts of will; and Lowes tended to depress the "Kubla Khan" situation to something *below* imaginative level. Coleridge's Preface seems to justify such treat-

[1] *BL*, I, 81.   [2] René Wellek, *Immanuel Kant in England*, p. 82.

ment, and there are many other passages in his writing which may superficially be quoted in support.

It is best to quote one of these first, to show the basis of Lowes's case, and the nature of the problem: this is again from the seventh chapter of the *Biographia*:

> Let us consider what we do when we leap. We first resist the gravitating power by an act purely voluntary, and then by another act, voluntary in part, we yield to it in order to light on the spot, which we had previously proposed to ourselves. Now let a man watch his mind while he is composing . . . and he will find the process completely analogous.[1]

Thinking and "composing" are essentially of the same kind. The imagination is operative in both, as being both active and passive. But in the composition of poetry there is operative a superior degree of the imagination "joined to a superior voluntary controul over it".[2] This is what is called in Chapter XIII the "secondary imagination".

According to the famous formal statement in Chapter XIII, in the working of the Primary Imagination the conscious will is not active: we all recognise that as a truth about our perception of the physical world. The fancy, as "a mode of Memory . . . blended with, and modified by that empirical phenomenon of the will, which we express by the word CHOICE"[3] we all recognise as a valid description of what happens when we try to write verses. But the relation of the Secondary Imagination to the "conscious will" is not so easy to grasp.

Coleridge must, of necessity, emphasise the *co-existence* of the conscious will with the Secondary Imagination in order to avoid the "mania" which is the final state of the Imagination "if the check of the senses and the reason were withdrawn".[4] In Chapter XIV of the *Biographia* he says that the power of the imagination is

first put in action by the will and understanding, and retained under their irremissive, though gentle and unnoticed, controul (*laxis effertur habenis*).[5]

---

[1] *BL*, I, 85.   [2] *ibid.*, 86.   [3] *BL*, II, 202.
[4] *Table Talk*, 23 June 1834.   [5] *BL*, II, 12.

This is a deliberately guarded, cautious statement of the matter. Dr. Richards was careful to make clear that "the empirical phenomenon of the will which we express by the word CHOICE", which is active in the operations of Fancy, "is *not* the will as a principle of the mind's being, striving to realise itself in knowing itself".[1] Is this, then, the will which remains "gentle and unnoticed" in the activity of the imagination?

At this point we can appeal for further light to a long passage analysing the workings of association which was not available to Dr. Richards when he wrote. It was first printed in 1940 in the article by Professor R. C. Bald to which I have already referred: he places it, hesitantly, in the year 1810. The focus of it, once more, is Sara Hutchinson, just as she was the focus of the Keswick meditation of 1803 and of the first version of "Dejection" in 1802. It carries further the analysis and the theorising of the experience which also underlies those two documents. For all its length, I must quote the whole of it:

I had been talking of the association of Ideas, and endeavoring to convince an Idolater of Hume & Hartley, that this was strictly speaking a law only of the memory & imagination, of the *Stuff out* of which we make our *con*ceptions & perceptions, not of the thinking faculty, *by* which we make them—that it was as the force of gravitation to leaping to any given point —without gravitation this would be impossible, and yet equally impossible to leap except by a *power* counteracting first, and then using the *force* of gravitation. That Will, strictly synonimous with the individualizing Principle, the *"I"* of every rational Being, was this governing and applying Power— And yet to shew him that I was neither ignorant, nor idle in observing, the vast extent and multifold activity of the *Associative Force/* I entered into a curious and tho fanciful yet strictly true and actual, exemplification. Many of my Instances recalled to my mind my little poem on *Lewti*, the Circassian/ and as by this same force joined with the assent of the will most often, tho' often too vainly because weakly opposed by it, I inevitably by some link or other return to you, or (say rather) bring some fuel of thought to the ceaseless

[1] Richards, p. 77.

yearning for you at my Inmost, which like a steady fire attracts constantly the air which constantly feeds it/ I began strictly and as matter of fact to examine that subtle Vulcanian Spider- -web Net of Stecl—strong as Steel yet subtle as the Ether, in which my soul flutters inclosed with the Idea of your's—to pass rapidly as in a catalogue thro' the Images only, exclusive of the thousand Thoughts that possess the same force, which never fail instantly to awake into vivider flame the forever and ever Feeling of you—The fire/ Mary, you, & I at Gallow- -Hill/ —or if flamy, reflected in children's round faces—ah whose children?—a dog—that dog whose restless eyes oft catching the light of the fire used to watch your face, as you leaned with your head on your hand and arm, & your feet on the *fender/* the fender thence/ —Fowls at Table—the last dinner at Gallow Hill, when you drest the two fowls in that delicious white Sauce which when very ill is the only idea of food that does not make me *sicker/* all natural Scenery—ten thousand links, and if it please me, the very spasm & drawing- -back of a pleasure which is half-pain your not being there— Cheese, at Middleham, too salt/ horses, my ride to Scarborough —asses, to that large living 2 or 3 miles from Middleham/ All Books—my study at Keswick/ —the Ceiling or Head of a Bed—the green watered Mazarine!—A Candle in it's socket, with its alternate fits & dying flashes of lingering Light—O God! O God!—Books of abstruse Knowledge—the Thomas Aquinas & Suarez from the Durham Library/ [1]

From this exceedingly interesting passage two things emerge, among much else, of special interest to Coleridge's theory and practice of poetry:

1. The stimulus and governing principle of the whole train of association is the affection for Sara, and the strong emotion accompanying it.

2. There is a rather fuller statement of the function of the *will* in the imaginative process than any given in the accounts which Coleridge himself published.

I will take these points in that order.

I inevitably by some link or other return to you, or (say rather) bring some fuel of thought to the ceaseless yearning for you at my Inmost, which like a steady fire attracts constantly the air which constantly feeds it. . . .

---

[1] Bald, pp. 23-4. Note-Book No. 18. Checked from Add. MSS 47515 ff. 10v-12.

This is one kind of the experience underlying colder statements in the published works. In a passage from the *Biographia* I have already quoted, Coleridge states as "the true *practical* general law of association" that "whatever makes certain parts of a total impression more vivid or distinct than the rest, will determine the mind to recall these in preference to others". A Note-Book entry, given in part in *Anima Poetæ*, expands and explains this:

O Heaven when I think how perishable Things, how imperishable Thoughts seem to be!—For what is Forgetfulness? Renew the state of affection or bodily Feeling, same or similar —sometimes dimly similar/ and instantly the trains of forgotten Thought rise from their living Catacombs! [1]

This statement that "affection and bodily feeling" become a focus-point for selective associating memory, must be seen in connection with the statement to Humphry Davy, in February 1801, that the book of poetry which should "supersede all the books of metaphysics and all the books of morals too" grew from the contemplation of "the affinities of the feelings with words and ideas" [2]; and also with his investigation of "the laws by which our feelings form affinities with each other and with words" [3].

Thus either "bodily feeling" or "emotion" (of which affection is the type) acts as a determining principle by which certain images or other material from memory are brought to the consciousness rather than others, and "feelings" in principle form affinities with "words and ideas". In some recent uses or adaptations of parts of Coleridge's theory, I think this emotional element has been given inadequate weight: "the balance or reconciliation of opposite or discordant qualities" has, in particular, been overworked in the interest of such effects as irony and paradox, and "the more than usual state of emotion, with more than usual order" has received less than its due share of attention. In fact, in

[1] Quoted in this form in Bald, p. 36; cf. *AP*, p. 8.
[2] *L*, I, 347.　　　　　　　　[3] Quoted *BL*, I, xxxi.

the famous definitions as they were published in the *Biographia* Coleridge had, in the attempt to reach formal, balanced completeness, pared away some of his own thoughts, almost to the point of leaving an inadequate residue. In particular, the emotional element had a far greater place in the earlier formulations of the definition of a poem by means of the antithesis between truth and pleasure.

This is apparent in the Lectures of 1811. There, after the statement of the principle of "the *communication of immediate pleasure*" [1], followed the attempt to distinguish "poems" from "novels, romances and other works of fiction" by means of the extra something which belonged to poems only—

that pleasurable emotion, that peculiar state and degree of excitement that arises in the poet himself in the act of composition.[2]

But this was not apparently his earliest formulation of the matter; for there are some interesting Note-Book entries that bear directly on it. I am not at all certain of their date, but incline to think they must have preceded the Lectures of 1811.

Dr. Richards acutely observed that Coleridge was in some way uneasy about the pleasure-truth opposition. "His numerous glosses and explanations show, I think, some lack of confidence about it." [3] This is borne out by the tentative formulations of the definition as they appear on page 230 of the Note-Book numbered 18.

I wish, I dared use the Brunonian phrase—& define Poetry—the Art of representing Objects in relation to the *excitability* of the human mind, &c—or what if we say—the communication of Thoughts and feelings so as to produce excitement by sympathy, for the purpose of immediate pleasure, the most pleasure from each part that is compatible with the largest possible sum of pleasure from the whole . . ?
The art of communicating whatever we wish to communicate so as to express and to produce excitement—or—in the

---

[1] *CSC*, II, 76.
[2] *ibid.*, p. 77, and cf., for the whole argument, pp. 66–9.
[3] Richards, p. 115.

way best fitted to express & to &c—or as applied to all the fine arts.

A communication of mental excitement for the purposes of immediate pleasure, in which each part is fitted to afford as much pleasure as is compatible with the largest possible Sum from the whole—[1]

It is clear, from these three formulations, that Coleridge was consciously and deliberately using the term "poetry" here in the first instance for a quality common to all the arts. Dr. Richards was unjustified in blaming him for using his terms evasively, to avoid the awkward consequences of his own definition; that he was fully aware of what he was doing is clearer still from the next page of Note-Book 18:

Many might be the equally good definitions of Poetry, as metrical Language—I have given the former the preference as comprizing the essential of all the fine Arts, and applying to Raphael & Handel equally as to Milton. But of Poetry commonly so called we might justly call it—A mode of composition that calls into action & gratifies the largest number of the human Faculties in Harmony with each other, & in just proportions. At least, it would furnish a scale of Merit if not a definition of *genus*. Frame a numerative table of the primary faculties of Man, as Reason, *unified per Ideas*, Mater Legum; Arbitrement [   ][2]; Judgement, the discriminitive; Fancy, the aggregative, Imagination, the modifying & fusive, the Senses & Sensations—and from these the different Derivatives of the Agreeable from the Senses, the Beautiful, the Sublime/ the Like and the Different—the spontaneous and the receptive, the Free and the Necessary—and whatever calls into consciousness the greatest number of these in due proportion & perfect harmony with each other, is the noblest Poem. Not the mere quantity of pleasure received can be any criterion, for that is endlessly dependent on accidents of the Subject receiving it, his age, sensibility, moral habits, &c— but the worth, the permanence, and comparative Independence of the Sources, from which the Pleasure has been derived.

This entirely justifies Dr. Richards's suggestion that

[1] MS Note-Book No. 18. Add. MSS 47515 f. 114v.
[2] Illegible in MS, possibly "Legibilitatis mater".

the kind of pleasure derived from poetry in its limited sense is to be understood in the light of what is said in the *Biographia* about the poet bringing the whole soul of man into activity. But the point I wish to emphasise here is that the "communication of thoughts and feelings so as to produce excitement by sympathy", which is common to all the arts, belongs also therefore to poetry in the narrower sense; and the thoughts and feelings are those which in the poet himself act as partly the stimulus and partly the controlling forces of the stream of his associations.

As an illustration of this in Coleridge's own work there could be no better example than "Frost at Midnight"; it is, as I said before, a poem *about* the movement of the mind; the movements are wide and the associations various; but they are all entirely under control, and the emotion which governs them is the affection for the

> Dear Babe, that sleepest cradled by my side.

I have never seen it suggested that "Frost at Midnight" is in any sense a dream poem or in any way affected by opium: it seems to be a plain case of waking association stimulated by one strong strain of feeling.

This brings us back to questions about the consciousness and the will and the different modes of association as between dreams and waking states. For the discussion of these there is no better reference-point than that unique monologue at Highgate on 11 April 1819:

> Nightingales, Poetry—on Poetical Sensation—Metaphysics—Different genera and species of Dreams—Nightmare—a dream accompanied by a sense of touch—single and double touch—A dream related—First and second consciousness—the difference explained between will and Volition—[1]

The listener and reporter was already the author of "Sleep and Poetry" and he went away to write the "Ode to a Nightingale": "do I wake or sleep?"

---

[1] *The Letters of John Keats*, edited by M. Buxton Forman, 1947, p. 324.

Anima Poetæ does not at all give a fair representation of the amount of space devoted to the description and discussion of dreams in Coleridge's Note-Books. The following extract is a sample, of three dreams, to illustrate the character of the entries:

October 3—Night. My Dreams uncommonly illustrative of the non-existence of Surprize in Sleep—I dreamt that I was asleep in the Cloysters at Christs Hospital & had awoken with a pain in my head from some ⌜corrosion¹⌝/ boys & nurses daughters peeping at me/ on their implying that I was not in the School, I answered yes I am/ I am only twenty—I then recollected that I was thirty, & of course could not be in the School, & was perplexed—but not the least surprize that I could fall into such an error/ So I dreamt of Dorothy, William & Mary—& that Dorothy was altered in every feature, a fat, thick-limbed & rather red-haired—in short, no resemblance to her at all—and I said, if I did not *know* you to be Dorothy, I never should suppose it/ Why, says she—I have not a feature the same/ & yet I was not surprized—

I was followed up & down by a frightful pale woman who, I thought, wanted to kiss me, & had the property of giving a shameful Disease by breathing on the face/

& again I dreamt that a figure of a woman of a gigantic Height, dim & indefinite & smokelike appeared—& that I was forced to run up toward it—& then it changed to a stool—& then appeared again in another place—& again I went up in great fright—& it changed to some other common thing—yet I felt no surprize.²

Professor Bald has shown, I think quite convincingly, that Coleridge recognised a whole range of different kinds of dream, day-dream and reverie.³ A well-known passage in Appendix B to *The Statesman's Manual* is here to the point.

Even *the visions of the night* speak to us of powers within us that are not dreamt of in their day-dream of philosophy. The dreams, which we most often remember, are produced by the nascent sensations and inward *motiunculae* (the fluxions) of the waking state. Hence, too, they are more capable of being

---

¹ This reading is doubtful.
² MS Note-Book No. 21. Add. MSS 47518, f. 41v.
³ Bald, pp. 37-43.

remembered, because passing more gradually into our waking thoughts they are more likely to associate with our first perceptions after sleep. Accordingly, when the nervous system is approaching to the waking state, a sort of under-consciousness blends with our dreams, that in all we imagine as seen or heard our own self is the ventriloquist, and moves the slides in the magic-lantern. We dream about things.

But there are few persons of tender feelings and reflecting habits, who have not, more or less often in the course of their lives, experienced dreams of a very different kind, and during the profoundest sleep that is compatible with after recollection,—states, of which it would scarcely be too bold to say that we dream the things themselves; so exact, minute, and vivid beyond all power of ordinary memory is the portraiture, so marvellously perfect is our brief *metempsychosis* into the very being, as it were, of the person who seems to address us. The dullest wight is at times a Shakspeare in his dreams.[1]

This is dealing with the differences between one kind of dream and another at a common and familiar level; but Coleridge's experience was various beyond the common, and he refined his knowledge of it. There is no doubt that his range of dream experience was largely due to opium. These opium experiences quoted in Professor Bald's essay [2] will indicate what is involved:

Purple *St[r]eams* in manifold Shapes, but angular—& then white or flesh-colored Streaks with Dark Streak/ or Dustiness streaked with Life & Flesh.

. . . but overpowered with the Phænomena I arose, lit my Candle, & wrote—of figures, even with open eyes/ of squares, & II, of various colours, & I know not what/

Then comes a day-dream, or waking run of association:

How in a few minutes I forgot such an Assemblage of distinct Impressions, ebullitions & piles of golden colour & thence to think of the Nature of Memory. So intense! & yet in one Minute forgotten! the same is in Dreams

Here we have what all of us, even without opium, can recognise, especially in fever—the impulse to write down, the inadequacy of what we write, the helpless

---

[1] *Lay Sermons*, ed. Derwent Coleridge, 3rd edn., 1852, pp. 84–5.
[2] p. 42. From MS Note-Book No. 16.

slipping away out of memory of what only a moment before had been so vivid. That is why we are not Shakespeares when we wake.

I do not want to diverge into the discussion of opium or the peculiar character of opium dreams, but to point out how Coleridge recognised certain types of dream-like experience which were not full dreams:

The Night-mair is not, properly, *a Dream*; but a species of Reverie, akin to Somnambulism, during which the Under-standing and moral Sense are awake, tho' more or less con-fused, and over the Terrors of which the Reason can exert no influence.[1]

It is well known that at one stage Coleridge put a sub-title to "The Ancient Mariner" and called it "A Poet's Reverie"; it was to this that Charles Lamb objected so strongly,[2] not recognising that Coleridge used the word "reverie" in an almost technical sense for a state which was different both from dreams and from normal waking consciousness. In contrast to this he found sometimes that his sleep approximated to ordinary waking states; he wrote to Tom Poole on 16 March 1801:

the sleep which I have is made up of ideas so connected, and so little different from the operations of reason, that it does not afford me the due refreshment.[3]

The recognition and examination of these intermediate states underlies, I believe, both Coleridge's knowledge that the "unconscious" plays a large part in poetic creation, and also his caution in formulating the description of the activity of the Will in co-existence with the Secondary Imagination.

Professor Bald follows Lowes in treating "Kubla Khan" as if it were a dream, and follows Abrams [4] in stressing the opium origin of it: but he goes further and finds more purely dream-like characteristics in "The Ancient Mariner" than Lowes did. And he does this with the

[1] Bald, p. 40 *n.* 4. From MS Note-Book No. 18.
[2] *Letters of Charles Lamb*, ed. E. V. Lucas (1935), I, 240.
[3] *L*, I, 349.
[4] Meyer H. Abrams, *The Milk of Paradise*, Cambridge, Mass., 1934.

implication that the phrase "pure imagination" deprives it of any serious content with reference to ethical and spiritual values, except in so far as it exemplifies the special activity of "the imagination".

While accepting Bald's facts, I put an entirely different interpretation on them. Starting from the belief that both "The Ancient Mariner" and "Kubla Khan" are poems which carry a great weight of important meaning—and indeed believing that they are only tolerable if they do—I conclude that Coleridge's intermediate states of "reverie" and states akin to them were the very experiences which underlay his description of the poet in creation as bringing the whole soul of man into activity. This is not to say that he believed that all poets in creation shared his own peculiar experiences; his friendship with Wordsworth would alone be enough to demonstrate that he did not; but that it was from these experiences that he reached the conception of an energetic unified personality directed in a single unifying creative act.

This is immediately relevant to the distinction which he made to Keats between "The Will" and "Volition". The Volition is what is active in the deliberate acts of conscious choice which go to the exercise of the Fancy, when in the act of composition selected items from the memory are brought into association as chosen "fixities and definites": the Will is, as it was described in the long Note-Book entry addressed to Sara Hutchinson, "strictly synonimous with the individualizing Principle, the 'I' of every rational Being" and is a "governing and applying Power" of quite a different order. This "real will" is active only when the "whole soul of man is brought into activity". Its material is not presented to the consciousness as matter of choice, but as being the realisation of an idea in a creative act: and the "idea" may only declare itself in the course of this realisation. I suggested that this was what happened in the course of the composition of "The Ancient Mariner"; and it was ultimately the failure to realise the "idea", which Coleridge spoke of as having dimly gathered from Crashaw's

Hymn to St. Theresa, which led to the collapse of "Christabel".

The control in composition is voluntary, just as a good man makes the right moral decisions from good habit and policy without need for reflection: he is spontaneously good. So the poet in creation creates spontaneously but not less, therefore, voluntarily.

As Wordsworth saw, the condition which Coleridge required for this spontaneous creative activity was a kind of happiness which health and his unfulfilled affections denied him. As the Dejection Ode itself made terribly clear, the essential Joy was missing. The controlling emotion which could unify the multiform findings of association, centred for the vital years of his life on Sara Hutchinson, was itself thwarted, impure and fitful: but he had enjoyed it enough to "unlabyrinth" the nature of the creative process in himself and others.

DEJECTION : AN ODE

THE following text of the earliest version of the poem is reprinted from *Wordsworthian and Other Studies* by Ernest de Selincourt (1947), pp. 67–76:

A LETTER TO——

April 4, 1802.   Sunday Evening.

Well! if the Bard was weatherwise, who made
The grand old Ballad of Sir Patrick Spence,
This Night, so tranquil now, will not go hence
Unrous'd by winds, that ply a busier trade
Than that, which moulds yon clouds in lazy flakes,   5
Or the dull sobbing Draft, that drones and rakes
Upon the Strings of this Eolian Lute,
Which better far were mute.
For, lo! the New Moon, winter-bright!
And overspread with phantom Light   10
(With swimming phantom Light o'erspread
But rimm'd and circled with a silver Thread)
I see the Old Moon in her Lap, foretelling
The coming-on of Rain and squally Blast—
O! Sara! that the Gust ev'n now were swelling,   15
And the slant Night-shower driving loud and fast!

A Grief without a pang, void, dark and drear,
A stifling, drowsy, unimpassion'd Grief
That finds no natural outlet, no Relief
In word, or sigh, or tear—   20
This, Sara! well thou know'st,
Is that sore Evil, which I dread the most,
And oft'nest suffer! In this heartless Mood,
To other thoughts by yonder Throstle woo'd,
That pipes within the Larch tree, not unseen,   25
(The Larch, which pushes out in tassels green
It's bundled Leafits) woo'd to mild Delights
By all the tender Sounds and gentle Sights

Of this sweet Primrose-month—and *vainly* woo'd
O dearest Sara! in this heartless Mood   30
All this long Eve, so balmy and serene,
Have I been gazing on the western Sky
And its peculiar Tint of Yellow Green—
And still I gaze—and with how blank an eye!
And those thin Clouds above, in flakes and bars,   35
That give away their Motion to the Stars;
Those Stars, that glide behind them, or between,
Now sparkling, now bedimm'd, but always seen;
Yon crescent Moon, as fix'd as if it grew
In it's own cloudless, starless Lake of Blue—   40
A boat becalm'd! dear William's Sky Canoe!
—I see them all, so excellently fair!
I see, not feel, how beautiful they are.

My genial Spirits fail—
And what can these avail   45
To lift the smoth'ring Weight from off my Breast?
It were a vain Endeavor,
Tho' I should gaze for ever
On that Green Light that lingers in the West!
I may not hope from outward Forms to win   50
The Passion and the Life, whose Fountains are within!

These lifeless Shapes, around, below, Above,
    O what can they impart?
When even the gentle Thought, that thou, my Love!
Art gazing, now, like me,   55
And see'st the Heaven, I see—
Sweet Thought it is—yet feebly stirs my Heart!

Feebly! O feebly!—Yet
(I well remember it)
In my first Dawn of Youth that Fancy stole   60
With many secret Yearnings on my Soul.
At eve, sky-gazing in "ecstatic fit"
(Alas! for cloister'd in a city School
The Sky was all, I knew, of Beautiful)
At the barr'd window often did I sit,   65
And oft upon the leaded School-roof lay,
And to myself would say—
There does not live the Man so stripp'd of good affections
As not to love to see a Maiden's quiet Eyes

Uprais'd, and linking on sweet Dreams by dim Connec-
tions   70
To Moon, or Evening Star, or glorious western Skies—
While yet a Boy, this Thought would so pursue me,
That often it became a kind of Vision to me!

Sweet Thought! and dear of old
To Hearts of finer Mould!   75
Ten thousand times by Friends and Lovers blest!
I spake with rash Despair,
And ere I was aware,
The Weight was somewhat lifted from my Breast!
O Sara! in the weather-fended Wood,   80
Thy lov'd haunt! where the Stock-doves coo at Noon
I guess, that thou hast stood
And watch'd yon Crescent, and it's ghost-like Moon.
And yet, far rather in my present Mood
I would, that thou'dst been sitting all this while   85
Upon the sod-built Seat of Camomile—
And tho' thy Robin may have ceas'd to sing,
Yet needs for *my* sake must thou love to hear
The Bee-hive murmuring near,
That ever-busy and most quiet Thing   90
Which I have heard at Midnight murmuring.

I feel my spirit moved.
And whereso'er thou be,
O Sister! O Beloved!
Those dear mild Eyes, that see   95
Even now the Heaven, *I* see—
There is a Prayer in them! It is for *me*—
And I, dear Sara, *I* am blessing *thee*!

It was as calm as this, that happy night
When Mary, thou, and I together were,   100
The low decaying Fire our only Light,
And listen'd to the Stillness of the Air!
O that affectionate and blameless Maid,
Dear Mary! on her Lap my head she lay'd—
Her Hand was on my Brow,   105
Even as my own is now;
And on my Cheek I felt the eye-lash play.
Such joy I had, that I may truly say,
My spirit was awe-stricken with the Excess
And trance-like Depth of it's brief Happiness.   110

Ah fair Remembrances, that so revive
The Heart, and fill it with a living Power,
Where were they, Sara?—or did I not strive
To win them to me?—on the fretting Hour
Then when I wrote thee that complaining Scroll,   115
Which even to bodily Sickness bruis'd thy Soul!
And yet thou blam'st thyself alone! And yet
Forbidd'st me all Regret!

And must I not regret, that I distress'd
Thee, best belov'd, who lovest me the best?   120
My better mind had fled, I know not whither,
For O! was this an absent Friend's Employ
To send from far both Pain and Sorrow thither
Where still his Blessings should have call'd down Joy!
I read thy guileless Letter o'er again—   125
I hear thee of thy blameless Self complain—
And only this I learn—and this, alas! I know—
That thou art weak and pale with Sickness, Grief, and
    Pain—
And I,—I made thee so!

O for my own sake I regret perforce   130
Whatever turns thee, Sara! from the course
Of calm Well-being and a Heart at rest!
When thou, and with thee those, whom thou lov'st
    best,
Shall dwell together in one happy Home,
One House, the dear *abiding* Home of All,   135
I too will crown me with a Coronal—
Nor shall this Heart in idle Wishes roam
    Morbidly soft!
No! let me trust, that I shall wear away
In no inglorious Toils the manly Day,   140
And only now and then, and not too oft,
Some dear and memorable Eve will bless
Dreaming of all your Loves and Quietness.
Be happy, and I need thee not in sight.
Peace in thy Heart, and Quiet in thy Dwelling,   145
Health in thy Limbs, and in thine eyes the Light
Of Love and Hope and honorable Feeling—
Where e'er I am, I shall be well content!
Not near thee, haply shall be more content!
To all things I prefer the Permanent.   150
And better seems it, for a Heart, like mine,

Always to *know*, than sometimes to behold,
   Their Happiness and thine—
For Change doth trouble me with pangs untold!
To see thee, hear thee, feel thee—then to part   155
   Oh! it weighs down the heart!
To *visit* those, I love, as I love thee,
Mary, and William, and dear Dorothy,
It is but a temptation to repine—
The transientness is Poison in the Wine,   160
Eats out the pith of Joy, makes all Joy hollow,
All Pleasure a dim Dream of Pain to follow!
My own peculiar Lot, my house-hold Life
It is, and will remain, Indifference or Strife.
While *Ye* are *well* and *happy*, 'twould but wrong you   165
If I should fondly yearn to be among you—
Wherefore, O wherefore! should I wish to be
A wither'd branch upon a blossoming Tree?

But (let me say it! for I vainly strive
To beat away the Thought), but if thou pin'd   170
Whate'er the Cause, in body or in mind,
I were the miserablest Man alive
To know it and be absent! Thy Delights
Far off, or near, alike I may partake—
But O! to mourn for thee, and to forsake   175
All power, all hope, of giving comfort to thee—
To know that thou art weak and worn with pain,
And not to hear thee, Sara! not to view thee—
   Not sit beside thy Bed,
   Not press thy aching Head,
   Not bring thee Health again—   180
   At least to hope, to try—
By this Voice, which thou lov'st, and by this earnest Eye—
Nay, wherefore did I let it haunt my Mind
The dark distressful Dream!   185
I turn from it, and listen to the Wind
Which long has rav'd unnotic'd! What a Scream
Of agony, by Torture lengthen'd out
That Lute sent forth! O thou wild Storm without!
Jagg'd Rock, or mountain Pond, or blasted Tree,   190
Or Pine-Grove, whither Woodman never clomb,
Or lonely House, long held the Witches' Home,
Methinks were fitter Instruments for Thee,
Mad Lutanist! that in this month of Showers,
Of dark brown Gardens and of peeping Flowers,   195

Mak'st Devil's Yule with worse than wintry Song
The Blossoms, Buds, and timorous Leaves among!
Thou Actor, perfect in all tragic Sounds!
Thou mighty Poet, even to frenzy bold!
What tell'st thou now about?   200
'Tis of the Rushing of an Host in Rout
And many groans for men with smarting Wounds—
At once they groan with smart, and shudder with the cold!
'Tis hush'd! there is a Trance of deepest Silence,
Again! but all that Sound, as of a rushing Crowd,   205
And Groans and tremulous Shudderings, all are over.
And it has other Sounds, and all less deep, less loud!
A Tale of less Affright,
And tempered with Delight,
As William's self had made the tender Lay—   210
'Tis of a little Child
Upon a heathy Wild,
Not far from home, but it has lost it's way—
And now moans low in utter grief and fear—
And now screams loud, and hopes to make it's Mother
   hear!

'Tis Midnight! and small Thoughts have I of Sleep.   216
Full seldom may my Friend such Vigils keep—
O breathe She softly in her gentle Sleep!
Cover her, gentle sleep! with wings of Healing.
And be this Tempest but a Mountain Birth!   220
May all the Stars hang bright above her Dwelling,
Silent, as though they *watch'd* the sleeping Earth!
Healthful and light, my Darling! may'st thou rise
With clear and chearful Eyes—
And of the same good Tidings to me send!   225
For oh! beloved Friend!
I am not the buoyant Thing I was of yore
When like an own Child, I to Joy belong'd:
For others mourning oft, myself oft sorely wrong'd,
Yet bearing all things then, as if I nothing bore!   230

Yes, dearest Sara, yes!
There *was* a time when tho' my path was rough,
The Joy within me dallied with Distress;
And all Misfortunes were but as the Stuff
Whence Fancy made me Dreams of Happiness;   235
For Hope grew round me, like the climbing Vine,
And Leaves and Fruitage, not my own, seem'd mine!

162

But now Ill Tidings bow me down to earth,
Nor care I that they rob me of my Mirth—
But Oh! each Visitation   240
Suspends what nature gave me at my Birth,
My shaping spirit of Imagination!

I speak not now of those habitual Ills
That wear out Life, when two unequal Minds
Meet in one House and two discordant Wills—   245
   This leaves me, where it finds,
Past Cure, and past Complaint,—a fate austere
Too fix'd and hopeless to partake of Fear!
But thou, dear Sara! (dear indeed thou art,
My Comforter, a Heart within my Heart!)   250
Thou, and the Few, we love, tho' few ye be,
Make up a World of Hopes and Fears for me.
And if Affliction, or distemp'ring Pain,
Or wayward Chance befall you, I complain
Not that I mourn—O Friends, most dear! most true!   255
   Methinks to weep with you
Were better far than to rejoice alone—
But that my coarse domestic Life has known
No Habits of heart-nursing Sympathy,
No Griefs but such as dull and deaden me,   260
No mutual mild Enjoyments of it's own,
No Hopes of its own Vintage, None O! none—
Whence when I mourn'd for you, my Heart might borrow
Fair forms and living Motions for it's Sorrow.
For not to think of what I needs must feel,   265
But to be still and patient all I can;
And haply by abstruse Research to steal
From my own Nature, all the Natural man—
This was my sole Resource, my wisest plan!
And that, which suits a part, infects the whole,   270
And now is almost grown the Temper of my Soul.

My little Children are a Joy, a Love,
   A good Gift from above!
But what is Bliss, that still calls up a Woe,
   And makes it doubly keen   275
Compelling me to *feel*, as well as *know*,
What a most blessed Lot mine might have been.
Those little Angel Children (woe is me!)
There have been hours when feeling how they bind
And pluck out the Wing-feathers of my Mind,   280

Turning my Error to Necessity,
I have half-wish'd they never had been born!
That seldom! but sad Thoughts they always bring,
And like the Poet's Philomel, I sing
My Love-song, with my breast against a Thorn.   285

With no unthankful Spirit I confess,
This clinging Grief, too, in it's turn, awakes
That Love, and Father's Joy; but O! it makes
The Love the greater, and the Joy far less.
These Mountains too, these Vales, these Woods, these
    Lakes,
Scenes full of Beauty and of Loftiness   291
Where all my Life I fondly hop'd to live—
I were sunk low indeed, did they *no* solace give;
But oft I seem to feel, and evermore I fear,
They are not to me now the Things, which once they were.

O Sara! we receive but what we give,   296
And in *our* life alone does Nature live
Our's is her Wedding Garment, our's her Shroud—
And would we aught behold of higher Worth
Than that inanimate cold World allow'd   300
To that poor loveless ever anxious Crowd,
Ah! from the Soul itself must issue forth
A Light, a Glory, and a luminous Cloud
Enveloping the Earth!
And from the Soul itself must there be sent   305
A sweet and potent Voice, of it's own Birth,
Of all sweet Sounds, the Life and Element.
O pure of Heart! thou need'st not ask of me
What this strong music in the Soul may be,
What and wherin it doth exist,   310
This Light, this Glory, this fair luminous Mist,
This beautiful and beauty-making Power!
Joy, innocent Sara! Joy, that ne'er was given
Save to the pure, and in their purest Hour,
Joy, Sara! is the Spirit and the Power,   315
That wedding Nature to us gives in Dower
        A new Earth and new Heaven,
Undreamt of by the Sensual and the Proud!
Joy is that strong Voice, Joy that luminous Cloud—
        We, we ourselves rejoice!   320
And thence flows all that charms or ear or sight,
All melodies, the Echoes of that Voice,

All Colors a Suffusion of that Light.
Sister and Friend of my devoutest Choice
Thou being innocent and full of love,   325
And nested with the Darlings of thy Love,
And feeling in thy Soul, Heart, Lips, and Arms
Even what the conjugal and mother Dove,
That borrows genial Warmth from those, she warms,
Feels in the thrill'd wings, blessedly outspread—   330
Thou free'd awhile from Cares and human Dread
By the Immenseness of the Good and Fair
   Which thou seest everywhere—
Thus, thus, should'st thou rejoice!
To thee would all things live from Pole to Pole;   335
Their Life the Eddying of thy living Soul—
O dear! O Innocent! O full of Love!
A very Friend! A Sister of my Choice—
O dear, as Light and Impulse from above,
Thus may'st thou ever, evermore rejoice!   340

S. T. C.

APPENDIX II

A NOTE ON "DEJECTION"

In dealing with the wind in "Dejection: an Ode" the
text of this book follows exactly what was said in the
lecture in March 1952; but since then I have had many
doubts and changes of thought, centred on line 129 of
the received text:

> And may this storm be but a mountain-birth.

I had long taken this to be a wish that what appeared
to be destructive might in fact turn out to be fruitfully
creative: but I am now almost convinced that the line
is a reminiscence of the famous one (l. 139) in Horace's
Ars Poetica:

> Parturient montes, nascetur ridiculus mus.

If this is so, Coleridge's line should be taken as a wish that
what seems to be terrible and destructive may turn out

165

after all to be a mere nothing, or a trifle that cannot disturb Sara's peace. The corresponding line in the original version (App. 1, l. 220)

And be this Tempest but a Mountain Birth

bears an exactly similar relation to the context; and this reading of the line must affect the interpretation of what has preceded. Stanza VII of the published version and lines 184–215 of the original version are virtually identical; and it now seems to me that the emphasis in them is not so much upon the creativeness of the wind (as Actor and Poet) as upon the evils, torments and sorrows which it appears to create. It still seems to me true that the vigour of this fierce wind (shown in the character of the verse describing the wind-made poems) acts as the stimulus to the lines on the Imagination, in that Coleridge's insight has been deepened by his response to it and by his development of the idea of its creativeness. But the relationship is not simple or direct. The matter is made more complicated by the fact that Horace's line is itself about the miscarriage or failure of poetic creation. "Be this Tempest but a Mountain Birth" then becomes a wish that the possible themes of the wind-as-poet (all terrible) may not be actualised so as to disturb Sara.

Furthermore, the relationship of mood to weather is, throughout Coleridge's lines, that which is summed up in the words "we receive but what we give". The possible wind-poems are thus possible Coleridge-poems; and there is involved the wish that he will not intrude with *his* "worse than wintry Song" upon the blossoms and buds of Wordsworth's spring-like creativeness. "I too will crown me with a Coronal" is a correlative wish to "be this Tempest but a Mountain Birth". The relation o. "Dejection" to the "Ode on the Intimations of Immortality" is too large a question to open up in a last-moment Appendix.

"THEODORUS CHERSITES"

AT the end of the first lecture, in February 1952, when I quoted Coleridge's original note of his source for the phrase "myriad-minded" I said the manuscript Note-Book read: "hyperbole from Naucratius' panegyric of Theodorus Chersites"; and I added that S. Theodore is "usually called Studita, rather than Chersites". I repeated this in the broadcast version in March. During the summer I showed Miss Coburn the typescript of this passage, to which I had then written a footnote mentioning two seventeenth-century works in which Coleridge could have found the phrases: I still thought the reading of the manuscript was "Chersites". Later in the summer, on the very day before she was to sail for Canada, Miss Coburn was following up an unpublished statement by Coleridge, in a letter of 1802, that he would "use Cave" for information about the Fathers. And there, in William Cave's *Scriptorum Ecclesiasticorum Historia Literaria*, she found adjacent articles on Theodorus and Naucratius, with a large part of the Panegyric, including all Coleridge's phrases, printed in the second of them (1688 edn., I, 509–13; 1743 edn., II, 8–11). Cave's article on Theodore opens: "THEODORUS, *Studites* à monasterio, cui praefuit, dictus, Patriâ Constantinopolitanus, natus est 759." Miss Coburn says she is sure the correct reading of the Note-Book manuscript is "Studites": I am now convinced she is right. She has laid the ghost "Theodorus Chersites" for ever. Is it not also possible that an imperfect memory of Cave's phrasing led Coleridge into calling Theodore a "Patriarch of Constantinople" in the footnote to the *Biographia*? Cave calls Naucratius "ineptissimus Encomiastes".